BUYING & SELLING A RESTAURANT BUSINESS

For Maximum Profit

By Lynda Andrews

The Food Service Professionals Guide To:
Buying & Selling a Restaurant Business
For Maximum Profit: 365 Secrets Revealed

Atlantic Publishing Group, Inc. Copyright © 2003
1210 SW 23rd Place
Ocala, Florida 34474
800-541-1336
352-622-5836 - Fax

www.atlantic-pub.com - Web site
sales@atlantic-pub.com E-mail

SAN Number :268-1250

International Standard Book Number: 0-910627-12-6

Library of Congress Cataloging-in-Publication Data

Andrews, Lynda.
Buying, selling & leasing a restaurant for maximum
profit : 365 secrets revealed / by Lynda Andrews.
p. cm. -- (The food service professionals guide to ; 2)
Includes bibliographical references and index.
ISBN 0-910627-12-6 (pbk. : alk. paper)
1. Restaurants--Valuation. 2. Restaurants--Finance.
I. Title.
II. Title: Buying, selling, and leasing a restaurant for
maximum profit. III. Series.
TX911.3.V34A53 2003
647.95'068'1--dc21
2002010831

Printed in Canada

CONTENTS

INTRODUCTION

1. BASIC REQUIREMENTS

Commonsense Thoughts on Selling 9

Consider the Practicalities -
      Don't Be Too Trusting..............................10

A Step Beyond Common Sense 13

Set Priorities and Proceed at Your Pace 15

Basic Selling Principles 18

Find Your Buyer 20

Your Job Is to Protect Your Restaurant -
      Other Considerations 23

The Transition - Get a Team in Place..............24

Get Your House in Order Legally 26

2. PREPARATION

Getting Ready for the Sale 29

Preparation - The Less Obvious Aspects..........31

More Steps to Selling 32

Putting Together a Winning Prospectus 34

The Prospectus: Don't Overdo It 37

Setting the Right Price 38

The Value of Other Assets 40

Beyond Real Estate - Other Pricing Factors 41

The Low-Down on Stocks 44

Just for Buyers 46

3. FRANCHISING

What about Franchising? 51

Advantages of Franchising..............................52

Disadvantages of Franchising 54

Franchise Financing 57

Evaluating a Franchise Opportunity 58
Franchising Checklist 59
Legalities Involving Franchise Restaurants 63
Living with the Franchisee/
    Franchiser Relationship 64

4. LEASING

Leases and the Start-Up Owner......................67
Ask Yourself the Question "Why Lease?" 69
Using a Lease Broker.....................................71
What Are the Benefits of Hiring a Broker?......72
Getting Yourself Ready to Lease......................74
The Power of Words 76
Changing the Face of Your Space 79
Clearly Define Who Does What 81
Understanding Your Lease Agreement 83

5. FINANCING THE DEAL

Where Will the Money Come From? 87
Getting Enough Money 90
Financing Made Easy 92
Other Ideas for Financing Your Restaurant 93
The Process of Due Diligence -
    General Considerations..............................95
Get to Grips with the
    Demands of Due Diligence 97
Making Money, Paying Taxes..........................99
Sale as Capital Gain? -
    Some Important Considerations 102
Closing the Deal 103

6. OTHER POSSIBILITIES

Going Through with the Deal -
    Should You Do It?.....................................107
Deciding Not to Sell 110
Closing Your Doors for Good? 113
Don't Make a Decision out of Embarrassment -
    Consider Alternatives 114
Selling Your Restaurant to an Employee 116
So, You Still Want Out? 118

7. ENSURING FUTURE SUCCESS

How Do I Project Future Sales? 123
Verify the Data..128
Service after the Sale 130
Advice for the New Proprietor.......................134
Closing Thoughts...138

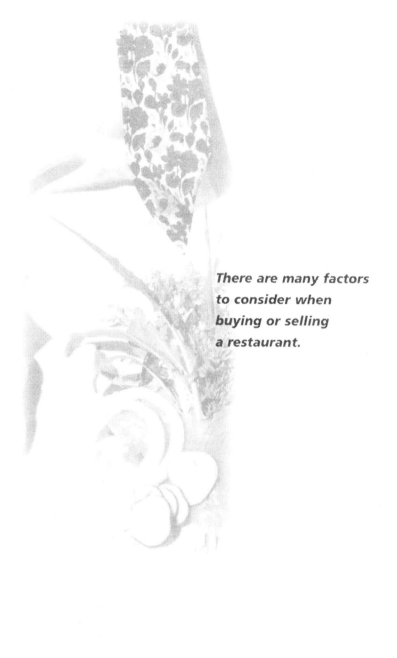

There are many factors to consider when buying or selling a restaurant.

INTRODUCTION

The buying and selling of a restaurant can become a very complex task with multiple considerations. In many ways, the purchase of a restaurant involves more arduous planning than that of other types of businesses because of the very nature of food service establishments.

This is not to say that other industries do not take on the personalities of their owners and employees. However, there is something about the food service experience that is very personal and fulfilling to its customers. We need only think back as far as the highly popular TV sitcom *Cheers* to get a wonderful picture of how patrons take on the personality of a restaurant or tavern. Many even find refuge from life in that very place. As a result, the owner of such an establishment cannot simply grow weary of long hours and sell out in a few short weeks or months. Selling a food service business is a complicated process and must be entered into with care, legal knowledge and great wisdom.

It is the intent of this manual to guide both the buyer and the seller through a process that can seem over-whelming and never-ending at times. Within these pages, you will also find valuable information on leasing restaurants. Leases affect a major sector of the restaurant industry, and a manual on buying and selling would not be complete without the addition of lease information.

Cheers!

Keep the business running right up until the last second.

CHAPTER ONE

BASIC REQUIREMENTS

Commonsense Thoughts on Selling

While selling your restaurant may involve detailed financial strategies or lengthy paperwork, there is a very sensible aspect to the whole idea of selling your business. Let's start with common sense. Consider the following:

- **Don't assume anything.** Remember, it's very easy to get caught up in the momentum of selling a business - just to have the deal fall through at the last minute. Nothing is certain until the last line on the contract is signed. Don't assume you've sold the restaurant unless everything is truly, legally finalized. Keep the business running up until the last second. If you run a restaurant with the anticipation of closing it, sloppy management can occur. These kinds of errors can be very costly in the long run. Don't slack on your diligence until the fat lady sings.

- **Commit yourself to investigating and exploring options.** Don't commit yourself to selling anything - not your restaurant, not a spatula, nothing. In your mind, simply promise yourself that you will explore your options. Jumping in too fast can be a mistake that will cost you thousands. Remember that your word may be seen as your bond. Don't shake hands or make promises until no rock is left unturned.

- **Be honest.** Being honest from the beginning can save more than face. It can save a business deal. Remember that it is better for a buyer to know unpopular or unflattering information up front. Problems that are uncovered late in a deal risk your reputation as a businessperson. They may also adversely affect the price you've agreed on. If shady dealings are uncovered well into the negotiations, the price may not be the only thing affected. You could see the entire sale fall through. So remember, honesty really is the best policy.

- **Have realistic goals.** Wouldn't it be great to sell your restaurant and make a huge profit? Sure, it would be nice, but not necessarily realistic. Or maybe your great dream is to sell the business in record time. Don't get discouraged if your timeline gets stretched a little. If you set your goals so high that they are unattainable, you'll most likely be disappointed. It's better to have healthy, realistic goals and see them come to fruition.

Consider the Practicalities - Don't Be Too Trusting

Okay, okay. So Joe is a great guy who has always wanted to own his very own restaurant. His credit report is clean, as is the space behind his ears. He's a great fellow and you all agree on the basic terms of the sale. You really want him to have this restaurant. Fine. But don't skip any necessary steps to make that happens. No matter how great this guy is, make sure every "i" is dotted and every "t" is crossed. It's just good business sense.

- **Double-check all your information.** Double-check all information before finalizing anything. Let's say you and Joe agree on everything regarding this business transaction. That doesn't mean all the information you agree on is accurate. It just means all you agree on is what information has been gathered to this point. You could all be agreeing on the same false, incomplete or inaccurate information.

- **Don't sign without reading - and understanding - first.** Think back to the first major purchase you ever made. Remember all those papers you signed? Did you really understand what it was that you were agreeing to do or pay? Did you really care? Sadly, many business transactions are handled without one or either party really knowing what they are signing. Make sure you fully understand what you are signing. Don't feel stupid; ask. If you still don't understand, ask until it is all very clear to you. Do not sign anything until you understand everything.

- **Remember the stock market.** Sell high, buy low, right? Keep that same mentality when selling your business. Too many business owners wait until business takes a negative turn before selling. In fact, it is wiser to sell when business is good. Sell on the upswing, not the downside.

- **Include past, present, and future assets in the deal.** Sellers include the past and present assets of their business when figuring the price on a deal. But the often-overlooked assets are those that may be more futuristic in nature. You should be able to document and illustrate, for interested buyers, the potential future earnings of the restaurant. You should profit on this future wealth as well as what's already in the bank.

- **Check the scales.** An important thing to remember when selling your restaurant (or any business for that matter) is the fact that sellers will probably be sellers only once or twice. Buyers make a career of it. That means, when selling your restaurant, you probably do not start out on an even playing field. Keep this in mind as you maneuver your way through this sale.

- **Select your attorney with care.** Don't choose a lawyer by flipping open the Yellow Pages with your eyes closed. Investigate and interview possible candidates for the position and spend time on this decision. An attorney can make or break the deal for you, so proceed with caution. Don't make this decision hurriedly. Choose the best lawyer for your individual situation. One possible choice is to select someone who is an attorney/CPA. This person will obviously cost more, but probably not more than hiring numerous professionals to be a part of your team.

- **If it ain't "quite," it ain't "right."** People make mistakes every day that they knew didn't seem to be right on target - especially the seller who is trying to finish up a business deal. It may not be good English, but if it ain't quite, it ain't right. No more needs to be said on this point.

A Step Beyond Common Sense

While common sense is the place to start with any business transaction, the successful seller must move beyond basic logic. The second level of selling expertise is only a rung or two higher than common sense, but it is the next necessary step to see a business deal through to the end. Consider some of the factors that will enable you to make the deal you've always dreamt of...and then some. Decide from the outset what your future role will be in the company. It is crucial for you to decide, at the beginning of the selling process, what your future connection will be to the company. Once your decision is made, don't go back on what you've said.

- **Question your role.** If you are a seller who simply wants to make a profit, then you're probably in the easiest selling position. But, if you intend to accept stock in the acquiring company, consider negotiating a management position. Give yourself some say in the future dealings of the restaurant. Decide up front what your role will be. A buyer is unlikely to give you more power down the road unless it is initially defined as a requirement of the sale.

- **Think of the buyer as your future boss.** Look at the buyer in terms of a long relationship. View the acquiring company or individual as a potential employer. Ask yourself a few hard questions: Would you work for this company? Would you be happy as an employee of this company? What kinds of stress would this employer add to your life? Would this be an easy employer/employee relationship? If the answers to these questions make you uneasy, get out of the deal now.

- **Don't expect the buyer to be a mind reader.** Keep in mind that your potential buyers are not mind readers. They do not have little crystal balls that allow them to see the years of information and experience that you have regarding your restaurant. Remember, you've watched the business grow. You know its real worth. Be patient with buyers who don't intuitively know what you do. You must effectively demonstrate the value of this restaurant to buyers in such a way that they begin to see its value through your eyes.

- **Think like a salesperson.** Maybe you've spent your entire life managing and owning a restaurant and you don't see yourself as a salesperson. Think back to how you sold the community on the catering aspect of your business, or how you sold your cafe as the perfect Valentine's spot. You have probably acted like a salesperson more than you realize. In order to really get top dollar for this business, you must present yourself and the business in the most positive light possible. That's going to take sales skills.

Set Priorities and Proceed at Your Pace

In any business deal, you will probably have many ideas of how you'd like this all to work out, but keep in mind that your potential buyer has a wish list as well. You probably will not get everything you want. Therefore, you must set priorities. Determine what the major issues are for you and set those aside as "nonnegotiable." In other words, these are the points on which you are not willing to compromise. Beyond these points, decide what the minor issues are from your perspective. Be willing to compromise on these. Determine your majors and minors before the negotiations begin. Consider the following:

- **It isn't over until the fat lady sings.** It's not over until the final second on the time clock runs out. When selling your restaurant, it's not over until every legal piece of the deal is completed. Remember that if the deal is not finished, it's not too late to walk away - even if you are down to the last few signatures. If you feel the sale is wrong, why not stop the lady from singing? You'll be glad you did.

- **Clean house.** Carry out any necessary repairs. If you were trying to sell your home, you would make needed repairs and do general house cleaning in order to present your home in the best possible condition to potential buyers. The same should be true for your restaurant. Don't fool yourself into believing that good buyers will be interested even if the place is a mess and needs painting and repairs. Spend the time and money necessary to put your best foot forward.

- **Develop good record-keeping skills.** Make a set of company accounts available for a prospective buyer. No individual or company is going to proceed with a purchase of your enterprise unless they are able to view accurate business records. Unfortunately, many private business owners keep less-than-perfect records. You want your restaurant to have the appearance of a well-organized company. That impression will be based in part on your record-keeping ability. If your records are a mess, the time to get your books in order is before going to market.

- **Keep them guessing.** Don't be a motor mouth. As the seller, you don't want to show your hand immediately. As a matter of fact, it is better to listen a lot and talk a little. The more you talk, the more you reveal about yourself and your motives. The more you listen, the more you learn about the potential acquirer and his motives. If there's any guessing to be done, let it come from the buyer. Use your ears more than your mouth.

- **Retain control in negotiations.** Depending on your personality and personal style, you may or may not want to be in every negotiating session. You may prefer to let your lawyers and staff handle much of the negotiation process. However, you need to be in control of what is happening at all times. If you are not present at all meetings, have a trusted associate attend for you and report directly to you. Make sure your interests and desires are being clearly and faithfully represented in all phases of the selling process.

- **Develop patience as a virtue.** Let's face it; selling a restaurant is a major undertaking. It's not like selling a car or even a house. It will take time. The seller who goes into the process knowing it will take time is less apt to be stressed during the process. The seller who has an unrealistic time frame in mind is more likely to get discouraged and sell short. Be determined to exercise patience.

- **Develop a sense of time.** There are some things you can control, like good record keeping and upkeep of your physical assets. However, there are numerous factors that will affect a selling price that you cannot control. For example, the stock market, current interest rates, bank lending policies, national economy and trends in industry will all affect the price you can ask for your restaurant. While you cannot control these factors, you can control timing. Select the time you will put your business up for sale according to a time that will be favorable to get the right price.

- **Learn to delegate.** That old mentality of, "I want it done right, so I'll do it myself," has gotten many a good man and woman into trouble. Buyers are often fearful that a company cannot survive without its current owner. If you can show that you have delegated authority and responsibility to a group of professionals who can successfully run this business after you're gone, the buyer will feel less vulnerable. However, if it is obvious that you do everything and even the least-significant decisions cannot be made without your input, buyers will most likely run from you. If you haven't already, learn to delegate.

Basic Selling Principles

Walk a mile in the buyer's shoes. What? Think like the buyer thinks? Walk in his shoes? Isn't my goal to secure the best deal for me? Well, yes and no. As a seller, you definitely want to solidify the deal that will represent your best interests. But one surefire way to obtain that is to make sure the other person is taken care of also. Some call it "win-win negotiating"; others may just call it good business sense. In this kind of negotiation, emotions must be kept in check. As a matter of fact, you must be willing to encourage participation and suggestions by the other party if you truly want a win-win situation. Consider the following:

- **View the buyer as a business partner.** One way to accomplish this is to adjust your mental picture of the buyer. Simple. Don't picture him or her as your adversary, but rather as a partner in a business venture.

- **Accentuate the positive.** And, yes, "eliminate the negative." In negotiating the sale of your restaurant, these words become more than lyrics. They are nuggets of wisdom that can be invaluable during the negotiating process. When you decide to sell your business, you simply must enter this sometimes-lengthy process with the thought of success. Believe that you will achieve the goals that you've set for this venture and then begin to work to see those goals realized!

- **Never, never, never, make a hasty decision.** Don't let yourself be pressured. If you are in a meeting where you are feeling "pushed" to make a decision now, follow this advice: don't do it. It is never prudent to make any major decision in haste. Quick decisions are usually not good ones. While you may hear the testimonial of someone who made a quick choice and gained incredible results, that is not the norm in the business world. If you're feeling pressured, end the negotiations. Walk away and schedule another meeting for another day. Make the decision that you will not be pressured into something that makes you feel uncomfortable.

- **If it seems too good to be true, it just might be.** If the thought that keeps coming to your mind is that this is simply too good to be true, beware! That tugging feeling in your heart or mind may just be the warning you need to back off and investigate exactly what the fine print does say. No more needs to be said here: if it seems too good to be true, it probably is.

- **Write down your goals.** Refer to them often. "Write the vision and make it plain." This is an old piece of wisdom, but a good one. In all the hassle and detailed negotiations, it is actually very easy to forget what your initial objectives were when you first started out in this process. You certainly do not want to get through the process just to realize that you didn't get any of your most important objectives met. Write them down and refer to them.

Find Your Buyer

Become Bond 007. That's right. In the initial stages of finding your buyer, think in terms of super sleuth. Bond, James Bond. Well, maybe you don't have to become 007, but keep in mind that it is a risky thing to announce publicly that your business is for sale. You don't want to lose business while trying to sell your business. So keep the sale under cover for as long as possible. Never lose sight of the following:

- **Auctions are risky.** Some restaurant owners may choose to auction their businesses, but this can be very risky. There are some things to be auctioned, others to be sold. If you do decide to go the auction route, hire a professional agent to handle it for you, and wear your rabbit's foot. You may need it.

- **Take the potential buyer out to lunch.** It is possible to let selected buyers know about your decision to sell in a private, discreet manner. If you choose to go this way, it is important that you get to know the people with whom you are dealing. Take them out to dinner or lunch. Spend quality time getting to know whether they are worth pursuing.

- **Try a middleman.** Some people swear by them, others would rather have nothing to do with them. Middlemen. Brokers, intermediaries, acquisition consultants - whatever you want to call them, they're middlemen. If you are awkward making contacts, a broker may be a good way for you to go. There are also other benefits of a man in the middle. Working with a broker allows you to take more time to think over proposals, allows you to make proposals that are not legally binding, and enables you to reach more possible buyers than you could probably contact alone.

- **Don't box yourself in with only one buyer.** Dealing with only one buyer is very appealing, to say the least. It presents fewer hassles, less work and, well, less competition. That's right. While dealing with one buyer may seem easier, you must realize that the buyer is in an ideal position, and you are boxed in when you limit your options so severely. Even though dealing with one person quietly may reduce certain risk factors, it also puts the buyer at a great advantage. Thumbs down on this idea.

- **Don't turn control over to a broker.** A broker is a definite asset when selling a restaurant, mainly because he or she can introduce you to more buyers than you could find on your own. However, remember that this is *your* restaurant. It's your sale. Don't turn the controls totally over to the broker. Hold onto the reins.

- **Be wary of a buyer-paid broker.** There are situations where buyers will pay for brokers. But let your suspicious genes flare up a little over the term "buyer-paid broker." Keep in mind that a broker paid for by the buyer will be on the buyer's team. You don't get something for nothing!

- **Utilize confidentiality agreements.** If you decide to employ the services of a broker, definitely use confidentiality agreements. Have the broker sign one, and keep the broker working within a very defined set of rules. He works for you and cannot proceed from one step to the next without your okay. It is especially imperative that you decide who gets data and information about your restaurant. You decide, not your broker.

- **A facilitator is a good listener.** A facilitator can listen to both sides and inform you regarding the bad and good points of each potential buyer. A buyer may talk more candidly with a facilitator than with you.

- **Your buyer might be right under your own nose.** Well, that's only true about 20 percent of the time. That's the percentage of times that a former or current employee purchases a commercial business, according to statistics on the subject. If the employee is someone well known to regulars, such as the bartender or headwaiter, it could be a comfortable deal - if financing is possible. However, it's important to remember that when these types of deals fall through, it can be very uncomfortable for everyone involved. Tread here with great care.

Your Job Is to Protect Your Restaurant - Other Considerations

Some buyers will begin demanding certain privileges or information during the negotiating process. Keep in the forefront of your mind that your restaurant must be protected throughout the sale, no matter what else fails. Don't be too hasty to accommodate a potential buyer. Protect the business now; it will pay off later.

- **Be cautious when using publications like offering memorandums.** This route can be a tricky one. It may get too much confidential information into the hands of too many people. Proceed with caution.

- **Disclose union information early in the process.** However you decide to get the information out and to whom, keep in mind the union issue. If yours is a union sale, make it known early. There are some buyers who simply will not close in such a situation, and there is no sense wasting time with them.

- **Competitors won't give you top dollar.** While competitors will probably show some interest in your restaurant, most information on this subject indicates that they will not pay top dollar for your business. If you're trying to make the most financially off the deal, your competitors probably will not become owners of your business.

The Transition · Get a Team in Place

Most buyers are wary of lost business during a transition. This loss of business can be especially true in the restaurant industry, where the owner's personality and connection to regular customers can surely play a part in business revenues. Ease the concerns of potential buyers by having a transition team assembled before the buyer has to ask about it. This will create peace of mind and a strong selling point for you to lean on.

Make your attorney work for you. Your attorney should represent what your goals are in this business transaction. Sometimes an attorney may start traveling down a road that you don't feel comfortable with; when this happens, it is up to you to apply the brakes. While your legal team means well, you need to be in control of what's happening. Remember, the transition is in your hands.

- **Choose your battles.** Always keep in mind that in negotiations there will be many battles. Choose yours wisely. If you insist on arguing over every point, you will probably not close any deal at all. Play up the fact that you are compromising on issues that really aren't major to you. That will give you leverage to ask for compromise on the things that really matter to you.

- **Prepare for closing early in the game.** If you get the offer you want, but are not ready, you risk losing the sale. Incomplete paperwork or other slowdowns can cause delay and even the termination of a sweet deal. Avoid such mishaps: plan ahead. Prepare early on as if you'll receive a dream offer tomorrow. Who knows? You just might.

- **Don't push too early for an offer in writing.** If you feel completely comfortable with a buyer and his offer, then you definitely want to get the offer in writing and sew the deal up as quickly as possible. Once an offer has been put in writing, it puts the seller on a type of timetable. It puts pressure on for you to make a decision. It also puts you in an awkward position with other potential buyers. The buyer who has made an offer on paper will most likely expect you to stop negotiating with other buyers. It boxes you in. Leave your options open to every possible buyer until you are ready to close. Resist the temptation to get it in writing if you are not ready to sign.

- **All they can do is say no.** If you are really going to get the best possible deal, you must not be afraid to ask. All they can do is say no. Too many potential sellers (and buyers) are afraid to ask for different proposals. First, forget about your reputation. Don't let fear of failure stop you from actively participating in the sale of your restaurant. Second, ask for specific additions or deletions from the deal, if that's what you want. It won't compromise the deal. Don't demand anything. But definitely ask.

- **Be willing to lose the deal.** It has been said that you must be willing to walk away from the deal in order to get the deal. There may be some truth in that thought. If a buyer sees you as desperate and willing to take whatever he offers, you won't control much of the dialogue. Instead, the buyer will control the entire deal, and you may be left to stew over what you didn't get. If, on the other hand, a buyer sees that you're more than willing to walk away from the table with no deal, he will be more willing to meet you half way. Be willing to lose the whole thing. It may get you exactly what you want.

Get Your House in Order Legally

Legal issues can make or break a deal. Tell the truth. This one simple piece of advice can save you more legal troubles than anything else. Just as you are expected to be honest when selling a house, you are really expected to be squeaky clean when selling a business. If you swear to tell the truth, the whole truth and nothing but the truth, you should be in good shape. Before proceeding with the sale, make sure that all legal requirements are in place. Consider the following:

- **Disclosure is more than a nice gesture.**
  Disclosure of facts relating to a sale is more than just a nice gesture on your part. It's a legal issue that you cannot avoid or ignore. No matter how damaging you think certain information might be, you must disclose all pertinent information. It's better to do so now than to face legal consequences down the road.

- **Buyers tend to be more negative than sellers.**
  Remember, it is you who knows all there is to know about the business in question. Fear of the unknown tends to make buyers a little more

negative than sellers. You should keep this in mind and truly endeavor to disclose all necessary information before the closing. As a matter of fact, disclose more than is necessary. It will save you a headache from a pessimistic buyer in future months.

- **Put it in writing.** Verbal conversations can always be disputed, but when something is put in writing it provides a permanent record. It is wise to put disclosures in writing so that there is no question in the future as to whether or not certain information was given to the buyer.

- **When in doubt, shout it out.** Okay, so you don't really have to shout. But, seriously, when you are in doubt as to whether or not a piece of information should be disclosed to the potential buyer, most experts agree that you should include that information in disclosure statements. If in doubt, disclose the information. Better safe than sorry.

- **Check and double-check all paperwork.** Make sure all legal documents are up to date and in order before beginning the selling process. It is very easy to get caught up in the day-to-day affairs of working in a small business and letting the legal documents gather dust. There are some documents that must be updated, filed and so on in the life of a restaurant.

- **Legal headaches are expensive.** As a buyer or a seller, don't fall back on the legal cushion instead of lining up all your ducks before closing. It's true that there are legal protections on both sides of the coin. But, those legal remedies are expensive ones. Sometimes, expense isn't only measured in dollars and cents. It can also be measured in loss of reputation, loss of business and so on. Do everything in such a way that legal expertise will not be needed later on.

- **Never sell or buy a restaurant without an attorney.** There are too many technicalities and details to close a sale without professional help. Never, ever, try to buy or sell a restaurant without the services of a qualified attorney.

CHAPTER TWO

PREPARATION

Getting Ready for the Sale

Be prepared to play the game. The seller must be prepared to list an asking price that is actually higher than what he expects to make because the buyer will always offer less than he is willing to pay. And thus the game begins. A seller should never go into this process expecting a quick sale, but rather should anticipate spending a year or more to see this through to the end.

- **Determine an asking price.** Set your asking price high. The seller will determine an asking price based upon a complete evaluation of the restaurant's assets such as inventories, licenses, personal goodwill and franchise affiliation.

- **Read a book on buying.** Believe it or not, you can learn a lot just by educating yourself on what the other side will be thinking. It doesn't make you a mind reader, but it does give you insight into how the opposite side will be looking at things. This can help protect you.

- **Plan on getting cash up front and leaving very little in escrow.** If you have a game plan going into the sale, you will have a little leverage regarding what you want out of this deal. One definite is to plan on lots of cash for you with little left in escrow. It is a very common practice for buyers to "bank on" getting escrow money back with indemnification claims. Avoid this pitfall of sellers by pushing for as much cash up front as possible, with as little left in escrow as you can swing.

- **Plan to require collateral.** If you plan to finance any part of the deal personally, be prepared to require collateral. However, make very certain that you will not be subordinated to a bank or another financial lending institution with whatever collateral you accept. For example, let's say you accept an office building and the surrounding acreage as collateral. Make sure no one else has a lien on that same property with you falling in line behind the other lender.

- **Determine who the buyer really is.** Sometimes your competitors may go on a little fishing expedition to gain access to your confidential information. Take the time to find out who this "buyer" really is. Make sure he's not a competitor with a Halloween mask.

- **Talk to other restaurant owners who were acquired by the same buyer.** Nothing speaks louder than experience. Gather the names of other owners who were acquired by the buyer you are interested in. Their experience will give you more insight than you could ever get from a good attorney or a book. And remember, if they turned out to be a disaster for someone else, chances are you could be next on their hit list.

Preparation - The Less Obvious Aspects

You should have an idea of what you're getting into before you get into it. One thing is knowing, realistically, how much you are going to spend in order to sell. Another is preparing yourself emotionally. If you are very emotionally wrapped up in the sale of this business, many statistics show you'll end up with less to show for it at the close of the sale. Try to be objective. That way, you'll end up with a better profit margin. Other, less obvious factors you need to consider include:

- **Broker fees.** Factor in all costs, such as the broker fee. For example, expect to pay a broker fee based on the Lehman Formula. Basically, this equals 5 percent of the first million, 4 percent of the second million, 3 percent of the third, 2 percent of the fourth, and 1 percent of the fifth million and any remaining balance.

- **Make sure any existing "Policy Manual" is up to date.** If something is in writing, it will be seen as the law of the land. Maybe you changed the policy years ago and your employees know it. You have to remember that the potential buyer doesn't know that. Any contradictions in what you tell him and what he reads in your policy manual can make him question your organization - and your honesty. If it's written down, make sure it's correct!

- **Pick the right time to sell.** Timing is everything! You may get the itch to sell at a time when the market will not yield the best return for your restaurant. Be patient enough to wait out the market and get in at the right time. Also, if there has been a continued downturn in your business, you definitely want to sell before you totally hit rock bottom. If you sell before you can touch the bottom, you can keep more of what you poured into those long restaurant hours.

- **Pick the right time to improve.** Don't spend one month totally fixing everything that you let slide for ten years, then put the business up for sale the next month. That's so obvious! Time your preparation for the sale up to three years ahead of time if possible. Make gradual changes that are not so obvious, but increase the value of the place at the same time.

- **Prepare financial statements.** Boring, yes. Tedious, yes. Necessary, yes. You simply must have current and accurate financial statements in order before you put your restaurant on the market. Don't even think about putting it up for sale until this is completed.

More Steps to Selling

Keep everything on a "need-to-know" basis. It isn't smart for you to tell everyone about the restaurant being for sale right away. Not even your employees. While some may feel that this is not completely honest, it is actually merciful. Employees who have knowledge of a pending sale get nervous. Everything is up in the air - including their jobs. You want your employees well rested. Don't let your possible sale keep them up at night. Keep mum on the subject except on a need-to-know basis. Bear in mind the following:

- **Present everything in a positive light.** When the big day comes that you must finally admit to employees, patrons and other business contacts that you are selling the business, it must be done in a positive manner. First, make it positive for them: their jobs are not in jeopardy; they will be taken care of; etc. Second, make it positive for you. Even if you have personal qualms about some specifics of the transaction, keep them to yourself. Keep everything positive.

- **Have a Plan B.** Some experts agree that the best weapon you can have in your arsenal is a Plan B. In other words, don't get yourself boxed in with one buyer, one financing plan and one game plan. Have another buyer in the pipeline or be fully prepared to keep the restaurant yourself. Let any potential buyer know that Plan B is a viable option.

- **Document the process.** Most successful businesses run on pure natural instinct. You know what you're doing in your establishment and you handle everyday crisis well. But prospective buyers need to know how you did it. Why? They need to be assured it will work for them too. Document your process as well as your policy.

- **Stay off the pages of the tabloids.** Once the news of your pending sale is made public, you should stay away from the tactics that get people's businesses smeared all over the pages of tabloid magazines. Tell people what you want them to know about this situation. If you don't tell them, they will get the information from somewhere. The only problem is, they may get less-than-accurate information out on the streets. Once a falsehood is spread, it's hard to get the correct information out there.

- **Don't cut corners when preparing your prospectus.** Now that you are ready to sell, you must prepare a sales prospectus (offering memorandum or marketing brochure) to inform potential buyers of the worth of your restaurant. This is probably the most important beginning step you will take toward selling your business, so don't make it cheap or inadequate. Do this part right.

Putting Together a Winning Prospectus

The prospectus should sell your restaurant for you. Your prospectus will most likely be read when you are not there to explain things that are unclear or not addressed. So that means there should be no unclear items or issues that are not addressed. When the buyer puts down the prospectus for your restaurant, she should want to call you immediately before someone else gets a jump on it. It needs to be that good.

- **Start out with a statement of opportunity.** Begin the prospectus with a tempting statement of the opportunity before this buyer. It should whet the appetite enough to make any buyer continue through the entire prospectus. You can win them in this section. Hire a professional writer if necessary; you cannot afford to lose them in this opening section.

- **Tell the history.** The buyer will want to know the history of your restaurant. In this section give information about the background of the restaurant, such as who started it and when, number of employees, annual sales, marketing niches and strengths, future goals and the basic reason the restaurant is now for sale.

- **Tell the location.** Include information about the general location of the restaurant. If, for example, your restaurant is in New York City, play on the obvious tourist industry and interest for restaurants in that city. This section should be brief and very vague.

- **Include an overview of sales and marketing information.** This should include everything from the company's marketing strategies to past successes and relationship with competition. A detailed analysis of every pertinent part of the marketing picture would be appropriate here.

- **Who are your employees?** Introduce the workforce. Provide general information about the existing staffing structure. Highlight key management figures in your organization. If you have a well-known chef on your staff, talk about the international magazines that have featured his recipes and the awards he has won. You can also talk about the pay scale you have in place and employee benefits in this section.

- **Sell unique and special assets.** Your restaurant may have special assets or licenses that no one else has available. You should outline any such assets in a special section. If it's an asset that no one else has, play it up. You're the only one who can.

- **Include financial statements.** Be prepared to include financial statements for the past three to five years. The buyer wants to know how much money he can make with your restaurant. Show him through your financial statements. You may want to include forecasts of future earnings, although you'll want to do so only with the okay of your legal counsel.

- **Tell them about the owners.** Include brief information that outlines exactly who owns the restaurant. If there are partners or shareholders, that should be stated.

- **Statement of caution.** While some do not recommend such a statement, it is probably wise to include a statement making potential buyers aware of the fact that patrons, employees, vendors and such are not aware of a pending sale. It could be beneficial down the road to have this in writing.

- **Name your price.** List your asking price with at least some explanation of how you justify that price. This should also be a section to outline very specifically any financing requirements. You can weed out buyers who will not agree with your financial requirements by being very candid in this part of your prospectus. Save yourself a lot of time negotiating with buyers who will never meet your terms.

- **Summarize the important points.** At the end of your prospectus, you'll want to have some type of summary available that basically outlines the opportunity presented. This conclusion should be well written, in strong language that will prompt the buyer to act. You may also want to include a statement giving the buyer information on how to set up a personal interview should she want to continue with her investigation of the restaurant.

The Prospectus: Don't Overdo It

Although the information provided in the prospectus is very important for getting your foot in the door with potential buyers, it doesn't have to include your life history. Actually, there are a few things you need to purposely leave out. The following suggestions will help guide you in areas where less is more:

- **Don't give them your address.** Although general location details must be included in the prospectus, make it very general. Don't give them your address. As a matter of fact, don't even tell them which city you're in unless your city is very large. Leave them guessing; otherwise, the whole neighborhood will know you're now on the market.

- **Don't give them your dirty laundry.** Some things need to be said face to face. There are those things that must be told, but should be told in the right way. If you have issues that may turn the buyer away while reading about it, hold that information until you meet in person.

- **Don't give them exact financial figures.**
  Important; DO include financial statements for
  three to five years. DO NOT provide actual
  financial documents and to-the-penny
  statements. Highlight the financial statements.
  You can get into the nitty-gritty later.

- **Don't give an inventory of every asset.**
  Provide highlights only. Remember, the
  prospectus should weed out those who really
  aren't suited for your restaurant and tantalize
  those who are. But it won't sell the business on
  it's own. Save the details for later.

- **Don't exaggerate.** Above all else, don't
  exaggerate the truth in your prospectus. Most
  buyers will see an exaggeration as a lie. For the
  right buyer, the whole truth will eventually come
  out, and when it does, you don't want to look
  like a liar. Avoid the temptation. Don't overstate
  the truth.

Setting the Right Price

In your prospectus, there will be a section that
declares your asking price. Many wonder, however,
just how do you reach an acceptable price? You want
a price that is not so high as to scare away good
buyers, yet, unless you're really in a desperate
situation, you want to make enough to have some left
over after paying all of your outstanding obligations.
First, when determining the value of a restaurant,
you must consider the actual real estate value of the
business (the actual land itself with any permanent
improvements such as parking lots, utility

connections, etc.). Many potential buyers will actually be more interested in the real estate than in the business itself. Therefore, it is important for a seller to know the true value of the land. The next several selling tips will involve determining the real estate value of your restaurant. We will begin with the three most common procedures for figuring the value of a restaurant: Market Approach, Cost Approach, and Income Approach.

- **Market Approach.** Market approach is based on the idea of substitution. This basically means that the value of a property is determined by comparing it to like pieces of property in similar areas. Adjustments will need to be made since your property will not be exactly like the property you are using for comparison. The most difficult part of trying the Market Approach is that owners of similar restaurants are probably not going to be willing to share specific details about their business with you.

- **Cost Approach.** Cost approach is based on the idea of replacement. Simply stated, the property is valued on what it would cost to replace it entirely. In order to do this, you must add all the replacement costs of all the assets in your restaurant. You can do this by obtaining purchase prices for new equipment and assets that exactly match your existing ones. Include all taxes, freight, etc., in your valuations. This approach is similar to practices used by insurance companies when processing a claim.

- **Income Approach.** Income approach bases its valuation on the anticipation of future income to be derived from the property. The real estate value, then, is the present value of the estimated future net income, plus the present value of the estimated profit earned when the property is sold. This is the preferred approach to use when figuring the value of your business.

The Value of Other Assets

The value of a restaurant basically consists of three different segments of assets: real estate, other reversion assets and the business itself. Reversion assets include assets that will retain their value even if the business fails. Examples of this might include antiques, inventories, receivables, licenses, etc. You can see that setting a selling price is not a cut-and-dry effort. There are many factors that must be considered. Here are just a few:

- **Profitability.** This has the most influence on the sales price and salability of a restaurant. The most common way to determine profitability is to examine the net operating income figure. If a restaurant earns an average net operating income, its most probable sales price will be equal to 50 percent of the previous 12 months' food and beverage sales. The net income should be compared to the industry standard for that type of operation, as well as to the regional standard.

- **Track record.** Buyers will be interested in restaurants that have a strong track record.

- **Leasehold terms and conditions.** The term remaining on the property lease and the monthly payment will affect the sales price greatly.

- **Goodwill.** The IRS determines goodwill as the amount of money paid for a restaurant in excess of the current book value of the physical assets. The best model to use for this process is the National Restaurant Association's annual Restaurant Industry Operations Report. You can obtain information about the association by visiting their Web site at www.restaurant.org. You may call them toll-free at 800-424-5156.

- **Personal goodwill.** If a large part of a restaurant's success is attributed to staff or management who will not be staying on, this can negatively affect the sale price.

Beyond Real Estate - Other Pricing Factors

Real estate value is only part of what goes into setting a price for your restaurant. Now we'll look at various other factors in the process:

- **Figure the value of likely future income and expenses.** This method for pricing your business relies on estimations or projections about the future of the company. If you are selling, you should estimate the future profits as high as realistically possible and expenses as low as possible. This will drive your asking price up. If, on the other hand, you are the buyer, you'll want to turn this formula around to drive the asking price down.

- **Figure the price based on comparable restaurants** (i.e., Market Approach). This method of pricing is very common with realtors who are selling homes. Simply stated, price is determined based on comparable houses that have sold in the area. Of course, negative and positive aspects specific to the house in question are factored into the price, but the basic idea is to compare the price with others in the same basic category. The same practice can be used with restaurants, but it will get a little more complex than figuring the asking price for a house. One kink in this method is that many sales of small restaurants will be kept private, thus it may be difficult to obtain pricing information about other (small) restaurant sales in your area.

- **Rule-of-thumb pricing.** One of the easiest ways to price a smaller restaurant (a restaurant with revenues under $5 million) is by a formula called rule-of-thumb pricing. Basically, you multiply the annual sales by a specific industry factor. This multiplying factor might, for example, be a percentage of annual gross sales. To determine the best multiplying factor at any given time for your restaurant, contact restaurant associations such as the National Restaurant Association at www.restaurant.org. They can help you to get started on the right track.

- **Use an appraiser.** One of the more accurate ways to determine an asking price is to hire a professional appraiser to figure the price for you. If you decide to go this route, be prepared to pay a fee of up to $10,000 for the services of the appraiser.

- **Keep the appraiser on a short leash.** Some appraisers require a fee based on the valuation of the restaurant or on the final sale price. Beware: If the appraiser's fee can go up or down depending on his or her own appraisal or on the sale price, you could end up with an appraiser whose motives aren't perfectly pure. Insist on a one-time flat rate. No exceptions.

- **Leave yourself room to negotiate.** Remember that in any business sale, the buyer will most likely want to negotiate. Include a margin of space to move around in the negotiation process. A good rule of thumb is to price your restaurant 10 to 20 percent above what you really want to make. This leaves you room to wiggle.

- **Understand the other guy's motive.** Here's a general rule to remember: Sellers are more driven by emotion in their pricing decisions; buyers are driven more by scientific reason and logic.

- **Unreasonable pricing and terms will kill the sale.** Keep in mind that if you have demands that a buyer sees as unreasonable, it will kill the deal. Some unreasonable or questionable requests might include extremely large cash down payments and all-cash demands. Be willing to compromise on what you think you should get. A little compromise avoids a lot of trouble.

The Low-Down on Stocks

Make sure you can sell any stocks acquired. When stocks are offered as part of the transaction, you must be very certain that you can actually sell the stocks and make money on them. Stocks can create the illusion that you are wealthy on paper, and, yet, provide you with no means to use your new "wealth." On top of the obvious downfall of such a transaction, you could also be liable to pay out a lot of money to cover your capital gains on this stock you now own. Consider the following:

- **Stocks will keep the seller involved.** This is a good position for the buyer. When stocks are involved as part of the purchase agreement, it keeps the seller involved to a certain degree, which is good for the new owner. What a seller must determine is whether or not she has any interest in staying connected to the company in this manner. It is a win-win arrangement for both parties in most situations. But if the seller wants to retire or totally refocus her business interests, she may not want to have stocks included in the transaction.

- **Exercise caution with stock options.** While transactions that include both cash and stock can be beneficial and profitable, they can also be faulty. The value that the buyer places on the stock must be in the same general neighborhood as where you, the seller, would place their value. Because of the complexity of such an agreement, it is highly recommended that you allow financial professionals to work out stock details for you.

- **Check out stock performance of the purchasing company.** If a publicly traded company makes an offer to purchase your restaurant, you must do a little sleuthing to see if you want to become entangled with the company. Check out the history of their performance in the stock market. If they historically have had a very low trading volume, you may end up with stock that is difficult to sell. In the long run, this may not be a good business venture for you.

- **Stocks do not represent a definite financial gain.** Bear in mind that the actual value of your stock really cannot be determined until a future date when you decide to sell the stock. As with any company on the stock market, the value of that stock may go up or down or remain steady. If you are considering stock as a large portion of the payment for your restaurant, you must be willing to live with whatever result emerges at the future sale of that stock.

- **Educate yourself on any possible restrictions to selling stock.** Many sellers assume that if they accept a stock agreement as part of the selling price of their restaurant, they will be able to sell that stock at any time. In most cases, this may be true. However, there may be some restrictions on when and if the stocks can be sold. Restrictions are sure to apply, at least to some degree, if the seller becomes an officer on the board of its purchasing company. If you are counting on the ability to sell your stock, you should educate yourself on the restrictions involved in such a venture before signing on the dotted line.

- **Investigate the purchasing company and their stock performance.** Check out their stock as if it were not a part of this purchase agreement. Would you invest in this company's stock if it were not a clause in your sales agreement? If you have to answer no to that question, you should also say no to any purchase that involves their stock as a part of your purchase price.

- **Buyers should pursue an asset sale as opposed to a stock sale.** Even if the offer sounds good, it is normally unwise to purchase restaurant's common stock rather than pursuing an asset sale. Although a stock sale may seem to provide overall savings and convenience in the short-term, future problems are likely to arise for the buyer. Go with the assets.

- **The seller may delay tax payments on the sale by accepting stock.** The biggest advantage to the seller in accepting stock in lieu of cash is the ability to delay paying taxes on the transaction. While each seller should check out the legalities involved in their specific sale, normally sellers who accept stocks for payment do not have to pay income tax until they actually sell the common stock. Many sellers see this as an advantage.

Just for Buyers

Just for a moment, let's consider some issues that only the buyer should know. Although the buyer will be putting out money to purchase this restaurant, there are ongoing expenses of owning a business. For corporations who acquire many businesses each year, this is not a revelation. But if this is your first venture into business ownership, particularly ownership of a restaurant, make sure you know what you are getting into. Financial disclosures and historical financial information should provide this information somewhere, but don't forget to include these secrets (expenses) in your long-term planning. Consider the following:

- **Payroll.** Although payroll is an ongoing expense, the restaurant industry has a plus in this area that many businesses wish they could realize. Many restaurants factor tips into the salary of wait staff, making the actual payroll for these employees very small.

- **Rent.** Rent takes a big bite out of monthly revenues. Depending on the kind of sale you are involved in, you may or may not end up with a rent payment. If you are buying the building and land as well as the restaurant, this will not be a factor.

- **Loan or financing payments.** Depending on how you have set up payments for the restaurant that you are acquiring, you will normally have some sort of financing or loan payment due each month.

- **Food.** Meat or seafood will most likely be the most expensive food item that you must buy each month. Make sure that current purchasing trends from the former owner are not excessive. Purchase all you need, but use all you purchase.

- **Other food items.** This includes everything from salad bar produce to desserts and garnishes. It should be said over and over again that you want to purchase enough so that you don't skimp on what you give the patron but keep costs reasonable.

- **Beverages.** This is an obvious expense. Let's beat the drum again: Don't waste it!

- **Beer, wine and other alcoholic beverages.** This will actually be one of the biggest bills you have if your establishment serves alcohol. It's lower only than rent, loans and food.

- **Bar supplies.** This expense includes everything from imprinted matchboxes and napkins to sip-sticks and straws. Buying in bulk will save you lots of dough.

- **Insurance.** Be sure to check with your attorney to see what kinds of insurance you need. Insurance payments may come annually, quarterly or monthly. While it may be tempting to let insurance payments slide when you're in a financial crunch, don't do it. Make sure your premiums are paid.

- **Attorney fees.** Obviously, if you're going to consult your attorney about insurance and other legal needs, you will have to pay that attorney for his or her services. Ouch!

- **Accountants and/or bookkeepers.** Some small restaurant owners try to cover this job themselves. A word to the wise: if you failed math in high school, hire an accountant. It's worth the investment.

- **Telephone, electricity, gas, water and other utilities.** You won't like paying the utility bills at work any more than you like paying them at home.

- **Licenses.** Depending on the location of your restaurant, these costs will vary. If you serve liquor, you will normally need a liquor license. There are also business licenses needed and, potentially, other possible such documents which vary from state to state. The good thing about this expense is that it will either be a one-time deal or an annual expense.

- **Exterminator.** Don't think you can skimp on this. Some states are very strict on their pest-control requirements for food service establishments. Hint: Some of the larger pest control companies offer incredible warranties for restaurants. They even have warranties that include calling the customer who saw a pest and taking full responsibility, including paying the customer's tab. These warranties are more expensive, but very impressive when you do have an unfortunate sighting.

- **Ongoing expenses.** Consider other expenses, such as cleaning supplies, bathroom items, décor improvements, linens, office supplies, etc., that must be taken care of continually.

Make sure the franchise can operate in your area.

CHAPTER THREE

FRANCHISING

What about Franchising?

You've decided you want to buy a restaurant, and you have done your homework. You understand all the costs and commitment involved. You've been shopping around for just the right place, but there's a question in the back of your mind about franchises. Would it be easier or more difficult to buy a franchise outlet? There are some significant advantages in the franchise system. Investigate some of the basics regarding buying, owning and maintaining a franchise restaurant:

- **Make sure the franchise you're interested in can operate in your area.** Although more than 200 of the franchise opportunities in the United States are restaurant franchises, that does not mean that all of them are registered and licensed to operate in every state. Before you start making specific plans, make sure the franchise you like is able to operate in your city and state.

- **Read the fine print.** Different franchise companies exert differing levels of control on their franchise owners. Don't take anything for granted. Read the fine print, then have your lawyer read it.

- **Buy into a success story?** When you buy into an established franchise, you are buying into a concept that (hopefully) already works. This is a definite plus for the franchise option.

- **Costs are lower.** One big advantage in choosing a franchise over a "from-scratch" restaurant is that the costs are much lower. If your funds are limited, a franchise may be your way to open a restaurant.

- **Risks are significantly reduced.** In the restaurant industry, you can significantly reduce your risks by buying into a franchise. Risks are there, but they are not as substantial as in starting your own restaurant. Americans like the familiar, and franchise restaurants are just that: familiar.

Advantages of Franchising

All of these factors can help increase your income and lower your risk of failure. As a franchisee you have the luxury of starting a business with:

- **Limited experience.** You are taking advantage of the franchisor's experience - experience which you probably would have gained the hard way: through trial and error.

- **A relatively small amount of capital and a strengthened financial and credit standing.** Sometimes the franchisor will give financial assistance to enable you to start with less than the usual amount of cash. For example, the franchisor may accept a down payment with your note for the balance of the needed capital. Or, the franchisor may allow you to delay in making payments on royalties or other fees in order to help you over the "rough spots." With the name of a well-known, successful franchisor behind you, your standing with financial institutions will be strengthened.

- **A well-developed image and consumer support of proven products and services.** The goods and services of the franchisor are proven and widely known. Therefore, your business has instant pulling power. To develop such pulling power on your own might take years of promotion and considerable investment.

- **Competently designed facilities, layout, displays and fixtures.** The franchising company has effectively designed facilities, layout, displays and fixtures based upon experience with many dealers.

- **Chain buying power.** You may receive savings through chain-style purchasing of products, equipment, supplies, advertising materials and other business needs.

- **The opportunity for business training** and continued assistance from experienced management in proven methods of doing business. You can normally expect to be trained in the mechanics of the restaurant business and guided in its day-to-day operations until you are proficient at the job. Moreover, management consulting services are provided by the franchisor on a continuing basis. This often includes help with record keeping as well as other accounting assistance.

- **National or regional promotion and publicity.** The national or regional promotion of the franchisor will help your business. Also, you will receive help and guidance with local advertising. The franchisor's program of research and development will assist you in keeping up with competition and changing times.

Disadvantages of Franchising

There are not only advantages associated with buying into a franchise, but some disadvantages as well. It is good to be well educated on the subject and to understand fully what you are buying into. Below are a few possible disadvantages to a franchise relationship:

- **Submission to imposed standardized operations.** You cannot make all the rules. Contrary to the "be your own boss" lures in franchise advertisements, you may not be your only boss. In addition, you must subjugate your personal identity to the name of the franchisor. Obviously, if you would like your operation to be known by your own name, a franchise is not for you. The franchisor exerts fundamental control and obligates you to:

  - Conform to standardized procedure.

- Handle specific products or services which may not be particularly profitable in your marketing area.

- Follow other policies which may benefit others in the chain but not you. This means that you forfeit the freedom to make many decisions; to be your own boss.

- **Sharing of profits with the franchisor.** The franchisor nearly always charges a royalty of a percentage of gross sales. This royalty fee must ultimately come out of the profits of the franchisee or be paid whether the franchisee makes a profit or not. Sometimes such fees are exorbitantly out of proportion to the profit. The report of a recent federal-government-sponsored study showed royalty payments in the fast-food franchising industry ranging from a low of 1 percent to a high of 18 percent of gross sales. The average royalty fee was 4 percent of gross sales.

- **Required purchases.** Merchandise, supplies or equipment that the franchisor requires you to buy from the corporation might be obtained elsewhere for less. The government study showed that in fast-food franchising many franchisees who were required to buy a large proportion of supplies from their franchisors were paying higher prices than they could obtain on their own. Additionally, you might pay more to the franchisor than other franchisees for the same services.

- **Lack of freedom to meet local competition.** Under a franchise you may be restricted in

establishing selling prices in introducing
additional products or services or dropping
unprofitable ones, even in the face of insidious
local competition.

- **Danger of contracts being slanted to the
  advantage of the franchisor.** Clauses in some
  contracts imposed by the franchisor provide for
  unreasonably high sales quotas, mandatory
  working hours, cancellation or termination of the
  franchise for minor infringements and restrictions on the franchisee in transferring the
  franchise or recovering his or her investment.
  The territory assigned the franchisee may
  overlap with that of another franchisee or may
  be otherwise inequitable. In settling disputes of
  any kind, the bargaining power of the franchisor
  is usually greater.

- **Time consumed in preparing reports required
  by the franchisor.** Franchisors require specific
  reports. The time and effort to prepare these
  may be inordinately burdensome. On the other
  hand, you should recognize that if these reports
  are helpful to the franchisor, they probably will
  help you to manage your business more
  effectively.

- **Sharing the burden of the franchisor's faults.**
  While ordinarily the franchisor's chain will have
  developed goodwill among consumers, there may
  be instances in which ill will has been developed.
  For example, if a customer has been served a
  stale roll or a burnt hamburger or received poor
  service in one outlet, he or she is apt to become
  disgruntled with the whole chain. As one outlet

in the chain, you will suffer regardless of the excellence of your particular unit. Furthermore, the franchisor may fail. You must bear the brunt of the chain's mistakes as well as share the glory of its good performances.

Franchise Financing

There are a growing number of alternatives for individuals and investors who want to enter franchising or expand their current market position. More and more local and regional banks, along with national non-bank lenders, are offering franchise financing. Lending institutions have a greater appreciation for the importance of franchising in the marketplace, for its future growth and stability as a distribution method.

- **The International Franchise Association** (www.franchise.org) lists more than 30 bank and non-bank franchise lenders in its Franchise Opportunities Guide this year.

- **The U.S. Small Business Administration** (www.sba.gov), which last year backed more than 60,000 small-business loans totaling $14.75 billion, works with local and regional banks to offer its guaranteed loan program to start-up franchisees.

Evaluating a Franchise Opportunity

A franchise costs money. One can be purchased for as little as a few hundred dollars, or as much as a quarter of a million dollars or more. Hence, it is vital that you investigate and evaluate carefully any franchise before you invest.

- **Beware of the "fast buck" artists.** The popularity of franchising has attracted an unsavory group of operators who will take you if they can. Sometimes known as "front money men," they usually offer nothing more than the sale of equipment and a catchy business name. Once they sell you the equipment, they do not care whether you succeed or fail. If you are promised tremendous profits in a short period of time, be wary.

The checklist on the next three pages will aid you in selecting the right franchise. Check each question when the answer is "yes." Most, if not all, questions should be checked before you sign a franchise contract.

Franchising Checklist

THE FRANCHISOR

☐ 1. Has the franchisor been in business long enough (five years or more) to have established a good reputation?

☐ 2. Have you checked Better Business Bureaus, Chambers of Commerce, Dun and Bradstreet and bankers to find out about the franchisor's business reputation and credit ratings?

☐ 3. Did the above investigations reveal that the franchisor has a good reputation and credit rating?

☐ 4. Does the franchising firm appear to be financed adequately so that it can carry out its stated plan of financial assistance and expansion?

☐ 5. Have you discovered how many franchisees are now operating?

☐ 6. Have you ascertained the "mortality," or failure, rate among franchisees?

☐ 7. Is the failure rate small?

☐ 8. Have you checked with some franchisees and found that the franchisor has a reputation for honesty and fair dealing among those who currently hold franchises?

☐ 9. Has the franchisor shown you certified figures indicating exact net profits of one or more going operations which you have personally checked yourself?

☐ 10. Has the franchisor given you a specimen contract to study with the advice of your legal counsel?

☐ 11. Will the franchisor assist you with:
  ☐ A management training program   ☐ Obtaining capital
  ☐ An employee training program   ☐ Good credit terms
  ☐ A public relations program   ☐ Merchandising
  ☐ Designing store layout/displays ☐ Inventory control
  ☐ Analyzing financial statements

☐ 12. Does the franchisor provide continuing assistance for franchisees through supervisors who visit regularly?

Franchising Checklist

☐ 13. Does the franchising firm have an experienced manager with in-depth training?

☐ 14. Will the franchisor assist you in finding a good location for your business?

☐ 15. Has the franchising company investigated you carefully enough to assure itself that you can successfully operate one of its franchises at a profit both to it and you?

☐ 16. Have you determined exactly what the franchisor can do for you that you cannot do yourself?

☐ 17. Does the franchise comply with all applicable laws?

☐ 18. If a product must be purchased exclusively from the franchisor or a designated supplier, are the prices to you, as the franchisee, competitive?

☐ 19. Does the franchise fee seem reasonable?

☐ 20. Do continuing royalty or percent-of-gross-sales payment requirements appear reasonable?

☐ 21. Are the total cash investment required and the terms for financing the balance satisfactory?

☐ 22. Does the cash investment include payment for fixtures and equipment?

☐ 23. If you will be required to participate in company-sponsored promotions and publicity by contributing to an advertising fund, will you have the right to veto an increase in contributions required?

☐ 24. Will you be free to buy the amount of merchandise you believe you need rather than a required amount?

☐ 25. Can merchandise be returned for credit?

☐ 26. Would you be free to engage in other business activities?

☐ 27. If there is an annual sales quota, can you retain your franchise if it is not met?

Franchising Checklist

❑ 28. Does the contract give you an exclusive territory for the length of the franchise?

❑ 29. Is your territory protected?

❑ 30. Is the franchise agreement renewable?

❑ 31. Can you terminate your agreement if you are not happy for any reason?

❑ 32. Is the franchisor prohibited from selling the franchise out from under you?

❑ 33. May you sell the business to whomever you please?

❑ 34. If you sell your franchise, will you be compensated for the goodwill you have built into the business?

❑ 35. Does the contract obligate the franchisor to give you continuing assistance while you are operating the business?

❑ 36. Are you permitted a choice in determining whether you will sell any new products introduced by the franchisor after you have opened your business?

❑ 37. Is there anything with respect to the franchise or its operation that would make you ineligible for special financial assistance and other benefits accorded to small-business concerns by federal, state or local governments?

❑ 38 Did your lawyer approve the franchise contract after he or she studied it paragraph by paragraph?

❑ 39. Is the contract free and clear of requirements compelling you at any point to take steps that are, according to your lawyer, unwise or illegal in your state, county or city?

❑ 40. Does the contract cover all aspects of your agreement with the franchisor?

❑ 41. Does the contract really benefit both you and the franchisor?

Franchising Checklist

YOUR MARKET

❑ 42. Are the territorial boundaries of your market completely, accurately and understandably defined?

❑ 43. Have you done a study to determine whether the product you propose to sell has a market in your territory at the prices you will have to charge?

❑ 44. Does the territory provide adequate sales potential?

❑ 45. Will the population in the territory given you increase over the next five years?

❑ 46. Will the average per capita income in the territory remain the same or increase over the next five years?

❑ 47. Do you know that existing competition in your territory is not well entrenched?

YOU—THE FRANCHISEE

❑ 48. Do you know where you will get the equity capital you need?

❑ 49 Have you compared what it will take to start your own restaurant with the price you must pay for the franchise?

❑ 50. Have you made a business plan? For example, have you worked out what income from sales or services you can reasonably expect in the first six months? the first year?

❑ 51. Have you made a forecast of expenses including your salary?

❑ 52. Are you prepared to give up some independence of action to secure the advantages offered by the franchise?

❑ 53. Are you capable of accepting supervision, even though you presumably will be your own boss?

❑ 54. Are you prepared to accept rules and regulations with which you may not agree?

❑ 55. Can you afford the period of training involved?

❑ 56. Are you ready to spend much or all of the remainder of your business life with this franchisor, offering this product or service to the public?

Legalities Involving Franchise Restaurants

As with any restaurant purchase, there is a legal and financial side that must be considered and understood as one moves toward the final decision to buy into a business. There are a few basics that you need to grasp before you can successfully maneuver your way into ownership of a franchise restaurant.

- **The Franchise Rule.** Ask your attorney to explain the Franchise Rule to you. The rule (named by and under the jurisdiction of the Federal Trade Commission) is the major item of regulatory rules for franchise operations in the United States. The next three ideas cover the three basic elements of the Franchise Rule. It is good for you to understand each one of them:

  - **Understanding the trademark.** The FTC law applies to franchises with a trademark, trade name, service mark or other commercial symbol, commonly known as "the mark." As a franchisee, you may be held to a certain standard of quality that is associated with that trademark. Please note that the FTC law does not cover businesses or franchises that do not have such a mark.

  - **Significant control or assistance.** As a franchisee, you should have assistance from your franchiser, but you will also experience certain controls placed on you and your restaurant by them. It is up to you to investigate exactly what these controls and assistance are in respect to your specific franchiser before entering into any legal contract.

- **Making the payment.** The franchisee will be required to pay the franchiser a sum of at least $500 during a time period starting before the opening of the franchise store to within six months of its commencement. This fee is a condition of the privilege of opening the franchise location.

- **Make sure the franchiser provides you with a disclosure document.** This document, sometimes called an offering circular, must be given to the franchisee ten days prior to the earlier of the two following situations: payment by the (potential) franchisee or the execution of a franchise contract or agreement.

- **Report violations.** As a potential or real franchisee, the Franchise Rule protects you. Certain violations carry with them a civil penalty of up to $10,000. Make sure you know the law or have an attorney who does. This law is in place to protect you; use it.

Living with the Franchisee/Franchiser Relationship

As with any business relationship, challenges can develop between the various parties, in this instance, the franchiser and the franchisee. In order to be truly successful as a franchisee, you need to understand the stresses that can creep into this relationship, the reasons for them and how to handle them. Consider the following:

- **Franchisee feels advertising is not effective.** In most franchise situations, there are strong controls and limitations on advertising that can and will take place. Franchisees often feel like the ads provided by the franchiser are not adequate and may cost too much. If you are in this situation, you should become part of a franchisee advertising committee in order to make real input about the problem.

- **Franchisees feel that they are doing all the work while the franchiser gets rich**. To be brutally honest, this is a problem of franchising that will never go away. While you may be doing "all the work," keep in mind that you did receive a business that was already laid out and successful. They deserve their fair cut, and you knew it before you signed up. You'll have to deal with this one.

- **Franchisers are not providing continuing assistance.** Keep in mind that a franchiser will provide certain services during the pre-opening stage that may not be provided later. Make certain that you understand which services were promised before and after your opening. If you are lacking services that you think should be ongoing, remind the franchiser of the written contract. Better still, have your attorney gently remind them.

- **Franchiser does not include franchisee in planning and pricing strategies.** If you as a franchisee feel that your voice is not heard loudly enough, let your franchiser know how you feel. Join franchisee committees that will give you a voice and show the franchiser that you are truly working for the good of the company. You should have input, and if you are persistent, your voice will be heard over time.

- **Expectations of the franchisee are not met.**
  Go back and reread the legal documents that
  were signed in this particular franchise
  agreement. If unmet expectations are legally the
  responsibility of the franchiser, then you need to
  alert your legal counsel to the problem. If you do
  not have a leg to stand on, legally speaking, ask
  for a meeting with the franchiser and explain
  your frustrations. Don't just present the problem;
  have some ideas for solutions ready when you
  meet with the franchiser's representative.

- **Purchasing requirements seem to be a
  moneymaking scheme for the franchiser.** If
  you feel like you are being required to purchase
  equipment and/or other items that seem to be a
  side business for the franchiser, you should
  check out your legal options. Are you bound to
  purchase the equipment from the franchiser?
  What does the original legal document say about
  the situation? Consult the franchiser and ask
  permission to purchase the equipment
  elsewhere. If the franchiser insists that their
  materials be purchased, ask why. There may be
  a quality issue, for example, that you are not
  aware of. Gather as much information as
  possible before making any major purchases.
  Document every conversation and purchase for
  future questions that may arise.

- **Franchiser institutes new controls not covered
  in the original franchise agreement.** Have your
  attorney check the fine print of the agreement
  contract you signed. Any unlawful controls
  should be challenged immediately with the proper
  attitude and through the correct legal channels.

CHAPTER FOUR

LEASING

Leases and the Start-Up Owner

In the business of buying and selling restaurants, it is important not to overlook leases and the issues they can present to any business owner. Take, for instance, the start-up restaurant owner who is looking to lease space for his or her restaurant, where the current owner is considering moving to a new location. Don't overlook the following:

- **Check any current leases before you begin searching for a new one.** If you already have space leased for your restaurant and you are looking to change locations, be sure that you check the lease you already have before looking for a new one. You want to time your new lease so that you are not hit with double rent payments. However, you don't want to wait until your current lease ends before beginning your search because your landlord might require you to sign a new lease so you'll stay put. Start looking several months in advance. Plan to start a new lease as close to the termination date of your current lease as possible.

- **Check out subletting options.** If your current lease gives you the option to sublet the property, you may actually be able to hold on to the current property and sublet it for a profit. This profit, in turn, can then be used to help pay the expenses on your newer, larger, better restaurant location. Have your attorney check the fine details so you can determine what may be right for you.

- **Ask about a buyout.** If you cannot or do not want to sublet the property and must leave before your current lease expires, ask your landlord about the possibility of a buyout amount. This is a negotiated or set amount of money that the landlord will take to let you out of your lease. Oftentimes, it is a lesser amount than what you would pay for all the remaining months on your lease.

- **Consider signing a long-term lease.** When shopping around for new space, you should plan to sign a long-term lease if possible. Because this will protect the new landlord as well as yourself, most landlords will be open to the idea. A long-term lease is a smart option.

- **Make your list; check it twice.** So, you've decided to opt for a lease (preferably long-term); now make a list of "wants" and "needs." Remember that when you buy a restaurant, you are actually paying for its ability to generate a profit in the future. Will this location still be good for you five years from now? Make sure all your interior and exterior needs are on the list. What about security, the neighborhood, pending road construction and parking? Make sure your list covers everything. Now, check that list twice so you'll have it in your mind as you go lease looking.

- **Try to have the landlord pay the broker's fees as part of the lease agreement.** Many landlords will pick up the tab for the broker's fees even if the broker was one that you hired. If you come down to two properties that you like equally, check out the landlord's position on broker's fees. If one will pay the fee while the other will not, that may make your decision easier.

Ask Yourself the Question "Why Lease?"

Before disrupting and moving your business to a totally new location, it is important that you ask yourself why you are making this move. Some reasons can be corrected sufficiently to allow you to stay where you are. Make sure your reasons for leaving are good ones. Any move or transition will most likely disrupt your business to a certain degree. Consider the following possibilities:

- **Constant change is not good for your business.** Bear in mind that if you sign short-term leases, chances are good that you'll be going through this moving process several times. That is simply not good for business. People who enjoy your eatery will come for the familiarity as well as the food. They don't want changes every year, so neither should you.

- **Talk to your customers.** If you really feel you must move the location of your restaurant, consider talking with some of your regular customers about it. Get their input. After all, you don't want to lose the strong customer base you've built. If moving to a particular area would cause you to lose half of your current customers, it wouldn't be worth the change. Find out what your regulars have to say about it and incorporate their ideas in your search for new space.

- **Put your cash into your restaurant instead.** Moving a restaurant is expensive, not to mention time consuming. (And don't forget that time equals money!) Also, anyone who has ever spent time looking for business spaces knows the focus and time it takes. If you are distracted from your work every few years to look for space, your business will suffer. Maybe you're better off staying put!

- **Ask your landlord for help**. Sometimes your reasons for leaving involve things that your landlord can help you with. Some concerns may even be covered in your current lease. For example, if the building is looking rough on the exterior, your landlord may be responsible for the maintenance and upkeep on the building. Check your lease and talk to your landlord. Chances are he or she would rather put out a little cash in some paint or siding than to have to begin the leasing process again.

- **Ask your landlord for more space.** If you have simply outgrown your current location, your landlord may be able to help. If there is an adjacent space available, you may be able to add this square footage to your current location. As a matter of fact, some lease agreements may actually give you first option on the space. Check the possibilities before you pick up and move somewhere else.

Using a Lease Broker

Just as a broker can be retained to find a restaurant to buy, the services of a broker can also be utilized when it comes to business leases and acquiring lease space for your restaurant. Make sure you hire a commercial broker who specializes in commercial leases. If the broker deals primarily with residential work, she will not have the expertise that you need in order to find the best possible deal. Likewise, if she works with commercial properties, but only does sales and never leases, she won't be much help to you either. Find the broker who works with commercial leases everyday. Also, consider the following:

- **Check out references before you retain a broker.** Find out if other clients of this broker were satisfied. The best question to ask is this: "Would you use this broker again?"

- **Have everything in writing.** More than one headache has occurred due to hiring a broker with less-than-pure motives. To avoid any kind of hassle down the road, make sure the broker signs a very detailed contract that covers all of his or her obligations to you. Have your attorney look over the contract to ensure that it covers all possible scenarios before you sign.

- **"Listing brokers."** In the same way that some brokers are paid by the buyer in a restaurant-buy situation, brokers can also used by the landlord in a lease situation. These brokers are called listing brokers because the landlord has listed the property with the broker. Restaurant owners who are looking for property should beware of listing brokers. They may be honest, upright and all that good stuff, but remember, they work for the landlord.

- **Hire your own broker.** Rather than working through a broker who is representing the interests of the landlord, it might be better to hire your own broker. True, it will add some expense to the whole lease process, but you'll have the confidence of knowing that the broker's loyalties are with you.

- **Stay away from dual agents.** Some states allow brokers to work for both the landlord and the tenant. In this situation the broker agrees to be neutral. This is good in the sense that you know he will not be working against you on behalf of the landlord. It is not good, however, because he cannot give you any professional advice. If you're going to use a broker, you might as well get all the professional benefits that go with a broker's service. Skip the dual agent agreement. It's not in your best interest.

What Are the Benefits of Hiring a Broker?

Now that you know the kinds of brokers who are out there just waiting to work for you, let's examine the benefits of hiring a broker who is working to find your perfect restaurant space.

- **A broker will save you a lot of time.** For time-starved restaurant owners, this may be the best benefit of using a broker. If a broker knows his or her job and the geographic area you work in, she will be able to save you countless hours. She will be able to weed out many possible lease spaces before you ever see them. The places that she does take you to will fit into your business plan. Now it's simply up to you to choose which location you like the most. Let your broker do the hard part.

- **Brokers will do the legwork.** A broker who is working for you will take care of lots of details. He will contact any professionals needed, such as property inspectors and space planners, as well as gather other operating data for you. Once again, this frees up your time so that you can continue to focus on your business while he does the hard work for you.

- **Acts as your negotiator.** If you think that, just because you're leasing space rather than buying it, you won't have to go through a tedious negotiation process, you couldn't be further from the truth. Many details are involved in a restaurant lease. Make sure your broker acts as your negotiator.

- **Explains the lease to you.** A business lease can be a very lengthy and detailed legal contract. Your broker has the expertise to explain the lease to you in terms you can understand. If you don't understand something, ask your broker before you sign. That's why you're paying her.

Getting Yourself Ready to Lease

Just as there are preparatory steps that you must take when you plan to buy a restaurant, you must also position yourself to get a good lease. If you are a landlord who is looking to lease your restaurant space, you'll want to secure the best possible tenant. Bear in mind the following issues:

- **Get your financial records in order.** The landlord will want to know that your business generates enough income to pay the rent on his lease space. You will need to be prepared to show the landlord current and historical financial records including bank statements. Don't make him have to ask for them; have them organized and ready to go.

- **Clean up your credit report.** If your personal credit has any blemishes, you'll want to clean these up as much as possible. Your personal credit will reflect on you as a restaurant owner. Obtain a copy of your credit report and begin working to clean it up today. The three major credit reporting agencies include:

  Equifax
  www.equifax.com 800-685-1111

  Experian
  www.experian.com 888-397-3742

  Trans Union
  www.transunion.com 800-888-4213

- **Have a copy of your credit report handy.** Now that you've cleaned up your credit report, keep one on file. Make it easy for the landlord to get the information he or she needs to expedite this lease.

- **Add a letter of reference to your file.** While you're setting up a file, go ahead and acquire a letter of reference from your current and past landlords. It always puts a potential landlord at ease to see a reference from someone in his or her position.

- **Keep a list of past landlords and their phone numbers in your file.** A potential landlord will want to know where you've leased in the past and how to get in touch with those landlords. Have that information available when asked. (They will ask for it.)

- **Business tax returns.** You need to have copies of the restaurant's tax returns available for the last two to three years. Add these to your "looking for a lease" file.

- **Personal tax returns.** We've already mentioned the fact that your personal credit will be under scrutiny. So will your tax returns. When copying the restaurant's tax returns, don't forget to include your personal ones as well.

- **Put a copy of your business plan in the file for good measure.** Be sure to include this in your "looking for a lease" file. It really helps the landlord understand your vision and long-term plans.

- **If you've got it, flaunt it.** A landlord is always looking for lessors who will bring goods or services needed by other tenants in the same building, shopping center or area. As a restaurant owner, you are in a strong position - so flaunt it. It really doesn't matter who leases the spaces in the shopping center around you. Remember, everyone needs to eat!

The Power of Words

Words can get us into big trouble in just about every situation one can imagine. When dealing with real estate issues, our words are especially powerful. Think carefully about the words you use with regard to lease letters of intent, as well as in the lease negotiating process.

- **Weigh the pros and cons of writing a letter of intent.** A letter of intent is a letter that is written after you and a landlord decide this may become a working relationship that benefits both of you. Basically, a letter of intent puts into writing the ideas and terms that the two of you agree to - in theory anyway. A letter can be initiated by you and your lawyer or by the landlord and his lawyer. There are pros and cons with regard to such a letter, and you should check with your attorney to see what is right for your individual situation.

- **A letter of intent can be seen as legally binding.** Although a letter of intent can be positive and beneficial in that it can set the stage for smooth negotiations, it can be very negative if it is seen as binding - you don't want to be bound to anything, yet. If you choose to write the letter yourself, make sure your attorney reviews it before you give it to the landlord. If your attorney writes it for you, read it yourself to make sure he or she is not committing you to something you don't agree with at this point.

- **Avoid any language that says you've agreed to something.** You may want to confirm that the landlord remembers what he or she has agreed to. But make sure you avoid phrases like "We agreed to..." and "Like we agreed on in our conversation..."

- **Read letters of intent from the landlord or her lawyer very carefully.** Go through any letter from the landlord with a fine-tooth comb. If she uses language that implies an agreement, you need to take action to ensure that everyone knows that you have not yet agreed to any specific terms. Send a letter of your own so that you have it in writing. State that you do not feel that a letter of intent is appropriate at this time and that, for the time being, you'd prefer to continue with further informal negotiations. Make very sure your language states that you have not agreed to or bound yourself to anything in her letter. Do this without being confrontational.

- **Make sure you can change terms in any lease.** Sometimes a letter of intent will specify that the landlord or his or her lawyer will draft the lease. Don't agree to anything that says the landlord gets to draft the lease. You want to be able to add and delete from any lease until you are comfortable with its contents and language.

- **Never let yourself get boxed in.** Make sure that you do not allow this to happen. It is advisable that an attorney or experienced broker help you through this process. What seems like nothing to you might be a legally binding statement.

- **Talk to other restaurant owners who lease their property.** Find out details about their personal lease situations. They may have stumbled upon problems with lease wordings or sections that they didn't see before they signed. If they can share this information with you before you sign, it might save you a few headaches later.

- **Talk to other restaurant and business owners who lease from this particular landlord.** Other business owners (not necessarily restaurant owners) may be able to share with you important facts about this particular landlord and how he does business. If you can get a heads up on this kind of dilemma, you can eliminate problems before they occur.

- **Go over every single point in the lease with your lawyer.** It should go without saying that you need a lawyer when leasing space for your restaurant. But just in case you're thinking about winging it: Don't do that! Now, you have a lawyer; go over every single point in the lease with him. Remember, he is a lawyer. However, he's not a restaurant owner. He won't know what's important to you unless you tell him.

- **Talk to your lawyer early on in the process.** Don't wait until the night before you're to meet with the landlord to select a lawyer. Many new restaurant owners want to do all the preliminary work on a lease themselves and just have a lawyer glance at it and say it's fine right before the signing. That's just not how it works. Involve your lawyer early in the process.

Changing the Face of Your Space

It is highly unlikely that you will be able to find a place to lease that looks exactly like you need it to look. Before you lease anything, you should be very clear on who will be responsible for alterations and improvements to the property. Investigate the following:

- **First things first.** You must get any agreements about alterations and improvements written in as a part of the lease. Make sure the language is clear enough that you will not have to prove your case at a later date. It should be self-explanatory.

- **Keeping what belongs to you.** Trade fixtures are additions to the leased building that you have purchased by yourself and that you have used as a part of your business. This is a tricky thing: If you have added anything to the structure that has become an integral part of the building, or would damage the premises to remove, the landlord could force you to leave it when you terminate your lease. Although there are some exceptions to this rule, the only definite way to protect your property is to write in a very detailed clause about trade fixtures. Be sure to get the help of a lawyer on this one.

- **Consider drafting a separate agreement regarding alterations and improvements.** Although it may be possible to add all alterations to the lease, if extensive changes to the property are required, you may want to consider drafting an entirely separate document to cover these changes.

- **Don't take anything labeled "as is."** If a lease agreement lists the building or space in these terms, you need to be wary. "As is" usually indicates that the landlord knows about problems with the structure. He is most likely trying to pawn the costs of those repairs off on you. This would even include problems that were unlawful. You would, in essence, be accepting the property in an unlawful state - meaning it would be your financial responsibility to bring it up to standards.

- **Make sure franchise requirements are covered in the lease.** If your restaurant is a franchise, keep in mind that the franchiser will have very specific instructions on how your restaurant must look. Some franchisers even have their franchises laid out down to where filing cabinets will go. You must make sure that the requirements you are bound to in your franchise agreement are covered in your lease agreement as well.

Clearly Define Who Does What

You need to make sure that "who is responsible for what" is very clearly defined in the lease agreement. Even if you think your conversations have been very clear, write it into the lease agreements. Alterations and improvements can be very costly, and you don't want to be hit with unexpected expenses.

- **You should expect the landlord to pay for all capital improvements.** Capital improvements are those that will forever change the property and increase its market value. Because the landlord would benefit from such improvements long after you're gone, he or she should incur the cost of such a change.

- **You should expect to pay for all non-capital improvements.** There will be alterations and improvements that you make solely for your restaurant, which no future tenant would benefit from or want. These are called non-capital improvements and you will be expected to cover their cost.

- **Planning for the cost of insurance is a smart move.** Many landlords will require that you carry several different types of insurance including the kind that will cover anyone who gets hurt while making structural changes to your restaurant. Even if the landlord doesn't require it, insurance is a smart move. It is highly recommended that a restaurant owner carry workers' compensation and liability as well as other kinds of insurance policies. Talk to your insurance agent and your attorney about the minimum amount of insurance you should carry.

- **The landlord should pay for any structural work done on a new building.** If the place you are leasing is brand new and building is ongoing when you sign the lease, you should make sure that you don't get stuck paying for part of normal construction that would take place no matter what. The landlord pays the cost of building his building. Don't let him slip some of these costs in disguised as alterations.

- **Consider adding a "liquidated damages" clause to your lease.** When a landlord is late in completing alterations and improvements, thus causing your opening date to be pushed back, you should be entitled to some sort of compensation. But you must make sure that your choice of compensation is included in your lease agreement. The liquidated damages clause defines a specific, predetermined sum of money to be paid to you if the landlord is late. There are some variations on this and some risks as well. Consult your attorney about what is right for your individual situation.

- **Another franchise concern.** If you are legally bound by a franchiser to open your restaurant on a specified date, you should ensure that the landlord is legally bound to that date also. This is especially true if he or she is doing some or all of the improvements or alterations to the property. If a late landlord causes you to miss a franchise-specified date, you should have the legal compensation already named in writing.

- **Plan for the future.** Improvements may be needed in the future in the form of maintenance and repairs. Be sure that you and the landlord come to some kind of agreement regarding whose responsibility maintenance and repairs will be. Have these agreements included in writing as part of the lease agreement.

Understanding Your Lease Agreement

In the lease agreement you sign, there will be numerous sections or clauses. Some of these sections are as simple as the names of the people entering into the agreement and the amount of rent that will be paid. The following defines some of the clauses that you may see in your lease agreement. It isn't an all-inclusive list of the clauses and sections in a lease agreement; it simply covers some of the more common clauses that you may be asked to include.

- **Alterations and Repairs.** If alterations and improvements are significant, you may want to draft a separate document to outline all of the details in this section.

- **Term.** The clause defines the actual term of the contract. In other words, it will define when the lease begins and when it ends. Make sure you totally understand when you will begin paying rent, especially if repairs or construction are ongoing.

- **Parking.** A restaurant should always have adequate parking. If your food is awesome, but parking is a major issue, customers may choose an eatery where parking is easier. Make sure adequate parking is available and outlined as such in the lease agreement.

- **Insurance.** This outlines the minimum amounts of insurance your landlord requires. Always check with your attorney and your insurance agent, as it may be wise to take out more insurance than your landlord requires.

- **Utilities.** This should explain for you how the utility cost is figured and if the landlord is responsible for any of these costs.

- **Subletting.** This clause defines whether or not you are allowed to sublet the space you are leasing. If you believe you may have a desire to sublet in the future, you may push for the right to do so as a provision in the lease.

- **Condemnation.** This clause explains your rights should the building you are leasing be condemned by local, state, or federal government agencies. You may think this could never happen, but make sure this clause is intact and protects you in the event that it does.

- **Defaults and Remedies.** The consequences if the landlord or you default on the lease agreement should be covered in this section. Read this carefully and make sure the penalty for a landlord defaulting is enough to cover your losses in such an incident.

- **Destruction.** This part explains what will happen to your lease agreement if part or all of the building is destroyed. If you live in an area that is prone to floods, tornadoes, hurricanes, earthquakes and other devastating natural events, you will want these possibilities covered here as well. Make sure everything is covered in writing.

- **Deposit.** This section lists the deposit(s) required by the landlord.

- **Hold Over.** If you get to the end of your lease and decide not to leave, this section will cover all the details of what happens next.

- **Use of Premises.** Read this section very carefully. It defines the parameters of how you can use your rented space. You must make very certain that the restrictions listed here do not interfere with the operation of your business. For example, if the lease states that no alcoholic beverages may be sold on the premises, yet your bar tab is a large portion of your income, you must renegotiate this issue before signing the lease.

- **Taxes.** This section defines, in detail, the taxes due with regard to the property and who pays them.

- **Ongoing Maintenance and Repairs.** This is a very important clause. If you sign a long-term lease in particular, repairs and maintenance are inevitable. It is vital that it is laid out ahead of time how they will be carried out, including who will be financially responsible for these issues.

- **Options.** This can cover everything from an option to buy down to an option to expand. If you outgrow your current space, this clause could prove to be very important in the future. Make sure it's worded to your advantage now.

- **Guaranty.** Some landlords may request that you have a guarantor who will agree to cover financial obligations should you falter. If the landlord requires this, the guarantor also must sign the lease.

- **Dispute Resolution.** This section outlines how disputes between you and the landlord will be resolved. Basically, this section is set up with the intention of keeping disputes out of the courtroom.

CHAPTER FIVE

FINANCING THE DEAL

Where Will the Money Come From?

Whether you decide to start something unique or buy into a franchise system, the biggest obstacle for many people is the start-up money. The following includes some of the most common sources for acquiring start-up funds:

- **Small Business Administration.** Consult the Small Business Administration (SBA). This federally funded program assists in providing security for a bank loan. If you're disabled or a United States veteran, you'll be on first base before you make the call. Visit the SBA online at www.sba.gov. This particular Web site has a wealth of information and is worth visiting.

- **The SBA and franchises.** While the SBA views restaurants as risky, it does consider franchises in a different light. Most experts say that franchises have a failure rate of less than 10 percent - a low rate when compared with other new businesses. If you're planning to open a franchise restaurant, the SBA may be able to provide the backing you need to get started.

- **Bank loans.** Banks and other financial institutions have similar thoughts to the SBA's regarding restaurants; they see them as high-risk. Banks will want major collateral, like your house, stocks, ect. They do not want to loan funds on leased property, and they see no security in loaning money to buy old or used equipment. Prepare the requests you have for your bank with these three guidelines in mind. If you decide to approach your bank for a loan, be prepared to:

- Have collateral ready - it's a pre-requisite.
- Buy your restaurant property - don't lease it.
- Buy new equipment, not used.

- **Financial institutions.** There are some financial and lending institutions that are not banks per se. They are avenues you may want to explore, at least. Such institutions, however, are likely to be as stringent as banks on issues of collateral and other requirements.

- **Savings accounts and patience.** If you are currently working with a steady income, it is possible to begin savings towards ownership of your very own restaurant. You'll need to put your money in an account that earns as much interest as possible, and plan to save for about ten years. Patience is the key. This is not to say that you could raise all the capital needed to start a restaurant in ten years. You could, however, raise enough to cause a bank to see you as a good investment. If possible, plan a budget that will allow you to raise $80,000 to $100,000.

- **Stocks, 401Ks and other paper money.** You'd be surprised at how much money Americans have "lying around" that they don't think about as real cash. You may have enough to get a bank to give you a second look. Go dig out all your old paperwork, make a few phone calls and see how much capital you can raise in a day.

- **Inheritance.** Don't go looking for someone to die so that you can start your restaurant, but if you happen to come into an inheritance, don't squander it. It may provide all the start-up money you need.

- **Partners.** Many businesses, including restaurants, are started with the help of a silent financial partner. In other words, they provide most of the start-up funds while you provide the manpower to get the job done. If you know someone or are related to someone who could handle the financial investment needed, you might consider approaching that person with the idea. Just one word of caution: Make sure everything is put in writing so there's no reliance on verbal agreements. Even if you have known this person forever, make sure everything is legal and in ink. It will save you a lot of heartache later.

- **Loan sharks.** All you need to know about loan sharks is this: stay away from them. You don't want a restaurant that badly. Period.

Getting Enough Money

Once you have an idea of where you might begin digging for gold, you should be very sure that you dig deep enough. Many restaurants and other small businesses fail simply because they did not have enough start-up capital. It's not okay to have some funding; you must have enough. The following list covers only some of the start-up expenses you can expect with your restaurant. Remember, many entre-preneurs fail simply due to a lack of adequate start-up funds. Plan ahead and make sure you're not short-circuited before you begin. Explore the different costs associated with buying your own business. Consider how you should include these in your purchase plans.

- **Down payment.** A buyer must be prepared to put down approximately 25 percent of the sales price as a down payment. Different payment arrangements and financing plans may alter this slightly, but on average, this is what you should plan to put down on your restaurant.

- **Closing costs.** We've all heard the horror stories of people who have scraped together every penny to buy a house, only to find that the closing costs were much more than they ever anticipated. Investigate now what your closing costs will be and plan accordingly.

- **Super-sleuth fees.** Don't hesitate. Probably one of the best-spent allocations of money, this is also probably the one expense that many buyers forego. Basically, this is the money spent to investigate restaurant/business purchase opportunities. Up front you may be tempted to skip this expense, but in the long run, it could save you a lot of money.

- **"Petty cash."** Call it operating cash or cash on hand. The bottom line is that you should plan to have on hand one half of 1 percent of the annual sales volume of the restaurant you are buying. For example, if the annual sales of the restaurant are about $1,000,000, you'll need at least $5,000 on hand at all times to maintain this level of sales.

- **Inventory.** Cash doesn't include inventory that you must have available. Figure on 1 percent of the annual sales volume in inventory.

- **Fees, fees and more fees.** When starting or buying any kind of business, you must plan for the incredible number of fees that must be paid. Everything from equity fees to attorney fees, franchise fees to accounting fees will need to be taken care of. And don't forget all the permits, licenses and registrations you'll be required to have - and to pay for - according to the laws of your specific state.

- **Deposits, deposits and more deposits.** With a business, the list is endless. Just remember, deposits require up-front cash, so plan ahead.

- **Taxes, taxes...well, you get the idea.** Don't forget state, federal and local taxes. The government won't forget, so you shouldn't either!

Financing Made Easy

Anyone who has ever financed a restaurant (or any other kind of business for that matter) probably would not describe the financing of such as "easy." However, there are different modes of financing available, and one will be the easiest for you. Okay, maybe it won't be easy, but there is a financing choice that is the most doable for you. Consider the following common financing options available to the small business entrepreneur:

- **Equity financing.** Capital that you put at risk in a financing plan is called equity. There are many different kinds of equity financing, but the most obvious is equity supplied by the buyer. You can have your attorney sit down with you and discuss possible equity options for you as an individual buyer. And you won't be alone. Somewhere in the neighborhood of one-third of restaurants in the United States are owned by a sole proprietor.

- **Venture capital financing.** One of the practices in place to help entrepreneurs along the way is firms making a business out of providing capital for start-up enterprises. They are venture capital firms and they will loan you money - to make money in return. If your restaurant is one with expansion potential, a venture capital firm might be able to help. Be forewarned, though. They will require specific parameters regarding the management of your restaurant. They want to see a fairly quick yield on their money.

- **Partnerships.** Partnerships should be included

as a valuable resource for acquiring equity and financing a business. General partnerships involve two or more partners who each will work actively in the business. A limited partnership or limited partnership syndication includes a general partner who is active in the managing of the restaurant and other partners who are "silent" investors. Check with your attorney to see if either of these partnership arrangements might be right for your situation.

Other Ideas for Financing Your Restaurant

Equity financing is only one method of making a business deal come together. Let's explore other ideas as you prepare to finance your restaurant.

- **Consider financing even if you have the cash available.** Having cash on hand in a business is not only nice, it's important as well. If you can get a good financing deal laid out, it might be wise to go with a financing plan and conserve your cash. Cash is like oxygen. You need it to survive.

- **Consider involving the seller in the financing.** Borrowing a portion of the purchase price from the seller is a good strategy for most buyers. The logic goes something like this: If a seller knows that he will be repaid based on the performance of the company after he leaves, this information will do one of two things (or both). First, it may keep the seller involved in the company, which can be very good for the consistent flow of business. Second, it will ensure his honesty during the sale.

- **Utilize convertible securities.** Convertible securities involve a complex system that actually may be good for both the buyer and seller. It involves payments being made during the life of the note that can be converted to stock toward the end of the loan. Check with your financial advisor to see if this would be a good option for you.

- **Offer stock from your company as partial payment.** As a buyer this presents obvious benefits, and can be a good idea for the seller as well. However, the seller should be aware of any restrictions on trading or selling the stock. Also, the seller should beware of accepting too much stock in the deal. Remember, cash is a necessary part of life.

- **Hire the seller.** If a buyer can work out a deal to have the seller continue in a management position for a specified amount of time and work the salary of such a position into the financing plan, this may be a good financing tool. The downside of this plan is obvious. Buyer and seller alike should make sure they can both work together in harmony if a seller-employee deal is struck.

- **Mix and match.** After considering all possible options for financing your restaurant, experiment with mixing and matching possible strategies. You can include "some of this and a little of that." Find the combination that makes the most sense for your financial situation.

- **As a seller, consider doing some legwork on the financing.** If you are the seller, consider doing early legwork on the financing. If you work ahead and get the business approved for financing, then a buyer must work only to get himself approved. This can make the sale of your business move along quickly and more easily once the buyer decides to go ahead with it.

The Process of Due Diligence - General Considerations

You've now determined that your sleep habits are fine, so you are going ahead with the deal. Or, if you happen to be the seller, your sleep has now been rescued because the buyer lets you know he or she wants to go ahead with it. While there may be some relief at this time, this period is a strange block of time where there is a tentative agreement, but technically no agreement. This is the desert of due diligence.

- **The starting point.** When does this strange time called due diligence actually begin? It begins when the two parties have reached an agreement in principle. At this stage, make sure that your lawyers are busy behind the scenes, checking out all the finer details and basically covering themselves (and yourself) should any unforeseen problems arise.

- **Understand that the playing field will not be level.** If you are the seller, it is very important that you understand the nature of due diligence. This is a period of time during the sale process that is usually positive for the buyer and negative for the seller. You must not ignore this fact. If you understand it, you can better prepare for it. If you are the buyer, make sure that your legal team is known for their productivity during due process. It can be a good time for you.

- **As a seller, you should perform due diligence of your own.** As a seller, use this period during which a tentative agreement has been reached to clean up things and get everything in order before the buyer uses certain pieces of information against you. It may cost you initially, but it's worth the price in the end.

- **Strengthen your confidentiality agreement.** While most buyers will be required to sign a statement of confidentiality in the initial stages of the process, that primary agreement may not be strong enough for this phase of the negotiations. Remember that during the initial phases of talks, the buyer had very limited access to your restaurant. During this stage, no stone will be unturned. Make sure the confidentiality statement covers everything...and then some.

- **Practice patience during due diligence.** If you are a seller, you and your staff will have to practice patience during this hectic phase. At times the buyer and his or her team will seem like a swarm of hornets that just won't go away. They will ask the same exact questions in twenty different ways from ten different people. But, just remember - the period of due diligence doesn't last forever. It only seems like it does.

- **Have a tension reliever ready at all times.** You

know ahead of time that due diligence will be a major pain in the neck, so have a plan of escape ready. Have a tension reliever ready at all times. Whatever works for you is what you should have available. You may think that you cannot afford the 30 or 40 minutes it will take to unwind and de-stress, but with this pending deal, you cannot afford NOT to relax.

Get to Grips with the Demands of Due Diligence

Be prepared for an open house. The process of due diligence can create headaches for the seller because all of a sudden, it will seem like your restaurant is hosting an open house every other day. Bankers, financial lenders and investors of all kinds will come out of the woodwork. If you plan ahead for this and have confidence that you are ready for your business to be opened up to all these people, you'll be okay. If you don't prepare ahead of time, you'll be very stressed. Don't sign an agreement in principle until you're ready for an open house.

- **Don't be too free with your time.** When a buyer asks for an extension of time during the due diligence, it may mean that he or she is having difficulty arranging financing. Don't be too quick to agree to an extension of time for the due diligence period. Remember that due diligence will usually benefit the buyer, not the seller. So, if you are the seller, carefully evaluate why the buyer wants an extension. If you are a buyer, try to work within the agreed schedule. It will make the seller suspicious if you need more time.

- **Provide audits if at all possible.** When the due diligence begins, the first things a buyer will want to see are the financial statements. If you have audits on hand, it will move this process along. Without audits, the buyer's accountants and legal team will have tons of questions and will want to see every financial number ever tabulated. If at all possible, do not let this period drag on forever. Your employees will clue in quickly and your business could suffer. Have audits available if possible. Also, if you are a seller thinking about selling in three to four years, begin having an outside firm audit your restaurant annually beginning this year. By the time you sell, you'll have three or four years of audits available to produce for the prospective buyer.

- **Have any questionable environmental issues resolved.** The environment is a major concern for anyone purchasing a business or property of any kind. Nobody is willing to purchase something blindly without investigating any possible environmental citations or problems. If you have had environmental issues, you need to be open about it now. Don't hide anything. The buyer will find out anyway, and you certainly do not want your integrity questioned. Be prepared for specialist environmental firms to check you out from head to toe.

- **Disclose everything about everything.** If you are the seller, you really must be prepared for full disclosure. It is in your best interest to do so now. Remember that when a buyer or his attorney uncovers data that you did not disclose, it can bring everything to a grinding halt. It makes the buyer question your honesty and also makes him wonder what else you have not told him. Disclose everything.

- **The flip side of disclosure.** The flip side of disclosure pertains to you if you are the buyer. If you are planning to purchase a restaurant and discover inconsistencies during due diligence, a red light should flash in your head. Of course, there's the possibility that it was an oversight on the part of the seller or his or her legal team. But, if you observe obvious misrepresentations of the truth or blatant lies, you may want to consider stopping the deal right now. If a seller has lied to you about one thing, there are probably more lies further below the surface. Advance with great care.

- **Do not cause any delays.** As a seller, you should be working to move the due diligence along as quickly as possible. You do not want this phase to stall or take forever. So, even if it means long hours and answering the same questions a hundred times or more, keep the process moving.

Making Money, Paying Taxes

As a seller, you may be thinking about all you want to do with the profit made on your restaurant. But you must keep in mind that any time you make money, there will be a tax bill to pay. Tax considerations should be kept in mind while you go through the process of selling your business. Although you may be at the very end of the sale process, don't think that it is too late to evaluate tax issues. Late is better than never.

- **Tax ramifications should be evaluated in any transaction.** Any time you are selling a restaurant or other business, keep the tax implications in mind. Don't let fear or disgust of taxes keep you from a making a great business sale, but do keep taxes in mind while walking through the process.

- **Get professional tax counsel.** Don't rely on your understanding of the tax code to make decisions. It may not even be wise to rely on an attorney for tax questions. If your attorney is not a tax specialist, you may want to consult someone who is before closing on any deal.

- **Making a total stock deal will not shelter you.** Some sellers mistakenly think that if they make a total stock deal, they will not have to pay any taxes on the sale. That's not strictly accurate. You will have to give an account of the increased (or decreased) value of the stocks you (now) own. This will need to be shown on either your personal or company's income tax return.

- **A loss could be a gain.** Interestingly, if a restaurant has a loss that must be carried over from previous years, the buyer can actually make a profit on that loss. For example, once the sale is complete, the buyer may then turn around and use your previous loss or losses as a deductible expense that he benefits from - yes, he is now making a profit from your loss! So, when figuring the selling price of your restaurant, you should actually figure those carried-over losses as an asset. You should add them in and make a profit on that loss as well!

- **Present the sale as a capital gain for the seller.** If the sale is presented as a capital gain for the seller, it should cause the income to qualify for a lower capital gains tax rate. This may benefit both the buyer and seller.

- **Avoid double taxation.** If you are the seller, you definitely want to avoid double taxation on the sale of your restaurant. There are two basic ways to do this. First, this can be avoided with the sale of an S corporation. The second way to avoid double taxing is to prepare the sale as a nontaxable transfer to the buyer.

- **Gamble with the future.** The seller can always opt to defer income from the sale to the future. The purpose would be to actually acquire the funds from the sale at a time when your tax rate is lower, thus decreasing the taxes owed. But this can be seen as somewhat of a gamble. This scenario might be a sure bet for the seller who knows without a doubt she will be retiring and falling into a lower tax bracket at a very definite time in the future.

- **Conform to IRS Code Section 368.** You'll want to make sure your tax professional works with you to enable you to possibly benefit from this IRS code. If you are in compliance with the code, purchases that involve buyer stock transactions might be tax-free.

- **Protect heirs.** If you are planning for the proceeds of this sale to belong to your heirs, you should talk to an accountant about the best way to protect them from taxes on their inheritance. An accountant and/or tax professional is the best person to talk to about this.

Sale as Capital Gain? - Some Important Considerations

If you are planning to present the sale as a capital gain to lower your tax rate, you should consider the pros and cons of such a maneuver. The following are pros of structuring your sale this way:

- **Assets sold can aid in the quest for capital gains.** Remember that any assets you sell (once you've had them for the minimum holding time of one year) are eligible to aid you in your quest for capital gains advantages.

- **The selection of assets to be sold is the option of the seller.** This is an option over which the seller has complete control. The selection of assets to be sold is the option of the seller. However, if the buyer is interested in your restaurant because of the incredible antiques that decorate your facility, don't expect him or her to agree to purchase the business without that asset. Don't let the sale of assets kill the overall deal.

- **Continuity.** Obviously, the selling business is allowed to continue its existence. This makes the possibility of selling the company and selling assets a real possibility.

- **Negative considerations.** There may also be negative aspects of maneuvering to get a capital gains sale. The following points address a few of these issues:

  - **The shareholder does not benefit.** While the seller will benefit from the sale of assets, the shareholders (if any) will not. As a matter of fact, shareholders may experience double taxation when asset sales proceeds are transferred to them.

  - **The individual seller benefits; the corporation does not.** As touched on before, when assets are sold to acquire a capital gains advantage, the individual seller may benefit, but the corporation does not.

Closing the Deal

Anyone who has ever worked a sales job knows that closing the deal is the greatest high you can get. Well, okay, maybe it's not that incredible, but it does create a release of pressure and a sense of accomplishment well worth savoring. If you've never closed on a business before, the following information will give you at least some idea of the minimum closing details to expect:

- **Have your legal team review the purchase agreement.** Don't sign any purchase agreement without reading it thoroughly. Then resist signing it until your attorney has read it. Why take such time with the purchase agreement?

An acquisition agreement is legally binding, and if you do not follow through with the terms outlined therein, you will be considered liable for damages.

- **Focus on the price and the terms of financing.** The most important aspect of a sale covered in a purchase agreement, obviously, is the money! Make certain that the price stated is the price you agreed to; do the same for the terms of payment. What you agree to here is how you will be paid. Make sure it's right.

- **Covenants.** Make sure that if your signing date and your closing date are different for any reason, you have the proper covenants in place to protect you during the "dead time." This is especially important for buyers. Covenants will ensure, for example, that the seller doesn't go out and incur thousands of dollars worth of debt during this void time. Covenants are extremely important; Make sure your legal team has included them and explained them to you.

- **Warranties and representations.** Both the seller and the buyer will be asked to make certain warranties and representations, but again, the seller is the one really in the hot seat. This means that it is the buyer who must be diligent to check out the representations put forth by the seller and ensure that they are carried out.

- **Indemnification.** The indemnification section of the purchase agreement is mainly for the protection of the buyer. The indemnification clauses basically outline the legal procedures that may be taken should a problem be found with the representation claims. Make sure this is in place, as it gives you legal protection.

- **Determine the best method for cash payments.** If you are a seller, you will need to decide beforehand how you want cash payments to be handled. Wire transfers are widely considered to be the safest and most sensible form of payment. Any other type of payment will most likely not provide immediate access to the cash, while a wire transfer would do so. Whatever you decide, familiarize yourself with your requirements beforehand.

Review everything carefully before closing the deal.

CHAPTER SIX

OTHER POSSIBILITIES

Going Through with the Deal - Should You Do It?

Let's look for a moment at things that the buyer should have at least considered before signing on the dotted line. Not to say that the seller isn't legitimate or honest, but the buyer is usually the one biting off a large financial obligation. "Caveat emptor" means "Let the buyer beware" or, more precisely, "Buyer beware." It may sound like a pessimistic view of humanity, but it is a good piece of advice. Not many people would buy a used car without kicking the tires, test driving it and possibly having a mechanic look it over. Why would you put any less investigation into the purchase of a restaurant that has much bigger financial risks? Consider the following:

- **Caveat emptor.** Beware of everything you've been told, read and shown. Beware. Be smart. Be alert.

- **Pause - step back.** By the time you actually sign the papers on a restaurant, you will have been involved in numerous and time-consuming negotiations. The seller may gradually introduce different ideas or conditions that you grow accustomed to the more you hear about it. It is possible to finally reach a "peace" about something simply because you are familiar with it. Don't let yourself be carried along with the flow. Step back. Talk to someone you trust. Take a break before you buy. Make sure you're not feeling comfortable with the purchase just because you are familiar with it.

- **Don't become too chummy with the seller.** A good working relationship is an important thing, especially if the seller will be involved with the restaurant after you buy it. However, becoming too chummy with the seller makes you vulnerable. The more she talks, the more she makes sense. Her position sounds good and you do like her, so, you end up with a deal you never wanted. Even if the seller is nice, honest and a reputable businessperson, his or her objectives may not line up with yours. Good doesn't necessarily equal what's right for you. Remember why you wanted to buy in the first place. If those objectives aren't met, don't sign. (The same is true for the seller: If your initial objections are not present in the final deal, junk it. You'll be glad you did).

- **Make a pros vs. cons list.** Do the old pros vs. cons list. Draw a line down the middle of a sheet of paper. On one side, list all the pros of the deal. On the other side, list all of the cons. If the pros substantially outweigh the cons, this might very well be a good move for you. If, on the other hand, the cons take great precedence over the pros, you might want to reconsider this business move.

- **Rank the deal on a scale of one to ten.** On a sheet of paper, write down all the major objectives you had when you started this process. After all the important objectives have been written down, go down the list and rank each from one to ten. A one means this business deal does not come anywhere near meeting the objective. A ten means it fulfills the objective perfectly. After ranking each separate objective, figure out the average. If your average score is a six or above, you will definitely want to explore the deal further. Proceed very cautiously with a five. Anything below a five should be stopped immediately.

- **Do you have to call before you visit?** Does the seller request that you call before you visit the restaurant? If he does, you should have the feeling that he is "getting ready for your visit" each time you come. That's not a good sign. If there is nothing to hide, you should be able to drop in at any time with little or no notice.

- **Watch for avoided questions or subjects.** Ever notice how politicians don't always answer the question? Businesspeople can be that way, too - especially if they're misrepresenting a business that they're trying to dump...er, sell. If there are pertinent questions or subjects that are always avoided, that should be a red flag for the buyer. If they won't answer, they're trying to hide something.

- **Ask other industry contacts about the seller and his or her management team.** It's always good to get references on anyone that you plan to deal with in a business purchase situation. Don't ask them for references, though; investigate, for yourself. Talk to industry leaders in the area. Also, talk to other business leaders in the area who are involved in businesses other than the food service industry. Ask blunt questions. Find out as much as you can about the seller's reputation regarding honesty and integrity.

- **Pay attention to your sleep habits.** As you move toward closing this deal, if you aren't sleeping well, put the insomnia into words. In other words, what are you worried about and thinking about that's keeping you awake? Whatever that worry is, that is what you must address before you finalize any purchase.

Deciding Not to Sell

One option that every seller needs to keep open is the option not to sell (as with the buyer who does not have to proceed with the purchase). It's far better to suffer the embarrassment of pulling out than to end up in a really bad situation. Remember, the seller has a right and an option to stop the process at any time. Bear in mind the following:

- **Get a realistic view of your asking price.** One discouragement to sellers is when they get offers that are way below their asking price. If this happens, you should find out if your price is, in fact, too high. Have a professional come in and evaluate your asking price. If you did set it a little (or a lot) high, are you willing to accept less? If not, you'd better roll up your sleeves; you've got a restaurant to run. If you are willing to accept less, work with the professional to set a more realistic price.

- **Find out why buyers aren't biting.** Do buyers seem interested, but they're not biting? Find out why. If the price seems right and all seems in order to you, you're obviously missing something - especially if you've had more than one interested buyer who didn't bite. Think about a buyer you developed rapport with; take that buyer out to lunch. Find out the reasons why he or she didn't buy. The best person to find out from is the one who got away.

- **Let bygones be bygones.** During the sale process, you probably let a lot of worms out of the can. Let those worms go. Many restaurant owners worry about how much they disclosed to potential buyers or key employees during the process. If anyone has a problem with the sale phases you went through, talk him or her through it honestly. If the buyer who got away uses information to hurt your business, outsmart him. But don't become obsessed with the process that didn't work. Get back to business as usual. The survival of your restaurant depends on it.

- **Put your employees at ease.** You will have to put your employees at ease. You must consider that they have dealt with stress, too, if they knew about your plans to sell. It's not easy thinking that you will have a new boss, not knowing if you will be kept on by the new owner, and so on. Your employees will not be feeling super-confident right now. It's your job to win their trust again.

- **Don't lose your customer base.** The restaurant owner has a great advantage over owners of businesses in other industries when it comes to taking that business off the market. Many customers of a food service establishment will actually be glad to hear you're not leaving, especially if you have a high goodwill rating with the community and your customer base. But while most will be relieved that you will still be there laughing and giving them specials on their anniversary, you may have some customers who are leery about your commitment to them and the business. Whatever you do, don't talk to them too much about the details of the failed sale. It's none of their business! Instead, work very hard to provide them with incredible service and extra perks during this period.

- **Watch for changes in relationships with vendors.** Some vendors, especially smaller companies, may be hesitant to offer you such lenient payment and credit terms as they once did. Simply stated, they don't want you to close up shop for good and leave them holding the bag. Make sure your bills are paid ahead of time and your dealings with them are iced in integrity. You can win their trust again, but remember, their business depends on you. It's natural for them to be suspicious for a while.

- **Considering liquidation.** If you realize that the right buyer did not come along but you still want out of the restaurant, you'll need to prepare yourself for liquidation of your company. It cannot happen overnight. You must develop a "game plan" to make the closing of your business as profitable for you as possible and fair for your employees.

Closing Your Doors for Good?

Once in a while, a seller will not find the right buyer, even though she really does want to get out of the restaurant business. Sometimes, closing down and liquidating is the right choice. Sometimes it's not. Never make a hasty decision about anything. It's just not good business. When reaching any decision regarding a total closeout, consider the following:

- **Motives.** First, look at why you want out. Examine and reexamine your motives for wanting to get away from it all.

- **Hire a manager.** The food service industry is unique with regard to the hours that one must work to be successful. If you love your restaurant and the revenues it brings in but are simply tired of the hours you work, consider hiring a manager. True, the additional salary will cut into your profits, but if you can afford it, this may save your restaurant. This may be a viable option for the restaurant owner who feels his family life is suffering due to long hours or the owner who is, simply, too old to continue. If the long and late hours are the main reason you want out, at least consider hiring a manager.

- **Take a vacation.** Maybe you don't need to

change your schedule permanently. Maybe you just haven't had a vacation in the last five years. Take a long vacation. Leave someone very capable in charge, and go. This may be all you need to get you pumped about your business again.

- **Learn to delegate.** Owning a restaurant can be a very high-stress, high-pressure job. The problem might not be that you need a manager or a vacation, but that you need to delegate to employees who are already on the payroll. Make a list of your job responsibilities. Now write down everything for which your key employees are responsible. Honestly evaluate these lists. Do you have trouble delegating? If so, make the decision to begin delegating immediately. This may provide the relief you need to really enjoy your restaurant once again.

Don't Make a Decision out of Embarrassment - Consider Alternatives

Too many business owners get embarrassed once their business has gone on the market and failed to sell. Some see it as a reflection on them personally or as a successful businessperson. If that's how you feel, get over it. Do not totally close the doors because of your pride. Your customers and employees really aren't making as big a deal out of this as you are, so stop obsessing about it and get on with life. Get on with your business.

- **Challenge yourself.** Think back to your original idea to sell the restaurant. Did it have anything to do with being restless and wanting a job change? It's natural to get bored with any job. The great thing about owning your own business is that you can change just about anything you want unless you are tied to a franchiser. If you don't have a controlling entity like a franchise, make changes that challenge you and your staff. Make changes that create a new, fun atmosphere to work and dine in. Basically, everything you've ever thought about doing, do it! Chances are, the business will profit from the changes, and your creative juices will begin to flow again. Go for it!

- **Create something totally different.** If you wanted to sell because the profit margin of your restaurant is just not sufficient enough to keep the doors open, consider rolling everything over into a new business venture. There is a very simple way to do this. Change the business address to your home address or a post office box (if your state will allow a P.O. box) so that the restaurant is still considered to be an existing business. Liquidate all the assets of the business and invest this cash in a high-interest-bearing account. When you are ready to start over again, this will serve as a great pocket of start-up funds for your new business or restaurant venture. Be sure to check with your legal and accounting professionals to ensure that you are complying with all the laws in your state that refer to this type of situation.

- **Give it away.** If you have a child or other heir who has shown interest in your restaurant at any time, consider giving it to him or her now as a part of his or her inheritance. Closing up for good is not as easy as it sounds. Many business owners say that they "grieved" over a closed business. If you think closing up would be hard for you, it might be easier to stomach if the restaurant continued on in your family. Don't think that just because he or she hasn't shown interest that he or she doesn't want it. Some kids feel like they cannot ask for something that isn't theirs. If you have an instinct she might be interested, talk to her about it. Let him know it's okay if he's not interested, but give him the chance.

Selling Your Restaurant to an Employee

If a sale is not forthcoming, think about selling the restaurant to a current employee. It's true that if you are a very small restaurant, this may not work for you. But then again, it might. Bear in mind that an employee often makes an excellent owner. The chef who has dreamed for years of owning her own restaurant and the head waiter who just got married and wants more out of his life are examples of good candidates. It also provides a way for you to make a real profit out of the place as well as keep your restaurant heritage alive! Consider selling to an employee under one of the following plans:

- **Management Buy Out** (MBO)
- **Leveraged Buy Out** (LBO)
- **Employee Stock Option Plan** (ESOP)

- **MBO.** Basically, this involves your management team guaranteeing a loan for the employee to purchase the company from you. Because the financing for such an arrangement is based on the financial performance of the company, this will only work if the restaurant can support the loan needed to make the transaction. Because the manager (or management team) is arranging the financing, he or she will normally be awarded about 30 percent of the company's equity when the deal is finished. This is considered to be a type of "commission" payment.

- **LBO.** This is similar to an MBO, but with a different financier. In this type of arrangement, a third party arranges the financing and splits the commission with the management team. In this arrangement, management would end up with not more than 10 percent commission.

- **ESOP.** With this type of agreement, your employees buy your stock as part of their retirement plan. This can be a good plan in that employees are more apt to work hard for a company that they "own." However, because it invests the employees' money almost entirely in the stock of this one restaurant or business, the employees take a great risk. If the stock takes a downturn, they could very well lose their profits. The ESOP route will only work realistically for restaurants with very large payrolls. If you should decide to go this route, there could be great tax incentives for you: If your company cannot be traded publicly; you use the proceeds to buy securities in American companies; you have had the stock three years or longer; and you've sold between 30 and 100 percent of shares to the ESOP, you may be eligible for a tax-free transaction. There are a few more requirements for such a perk, so check with your tax professional to see how you can qualify.

So, You Still Want Out?

If, after all the considerations about selling your restaurant, you still want out, first make sure you are completely ready to do this. Do it right so that there are no regrets in the future. Take time to develop a plan. You didn't expect to sell your restaurant overnight, and you should not expect to close it overnight. Many think of closing a business as a split-second decision that takes effect very quickly. If you are already at this point, you know yourself it wasn't a split-second decision. You have probably agonized over this for a long time. The second part of this is that it will not take effect quickly. You need to develop a plan that will allow you the most return on your investment dollars. You'll want to use up as much food and beverage inventory as possible so as to have no wasted food dollars, and you'll want to develop a closeout plan that is fair for your employees. Who knows? You may want to start another business in this community one day; you don't want the reputation of someone who made 20 people jobless, with no warning or provision for them. You should know up front that it usually takes months - sometimes years - to totally close up and liquidate a business. As you close the doors on your restaurant for good, consider the following:

- **Make a list of all liens.** You need to make a list of all the assets your restaurant has that have liens attached to them. If you decide to liquidate these assets by selling them, you'll need to select an asking price that will cover the amount you still owe your creditor. You definitely don't want to get out of business with thousands of dollars of liens to be paid off. If you have to take a hit on one asset, try to make it up by asking a little more on an asset that will sell for more.

- **Consider a liquidating professional if you aren't concerned with price.** If you are in a financial position where you really do not have to worry about how much you sell assets for, consider having a professional liquidator come in and take assets off your hands. Maybe you've heard of an estate buyer (someone who buys entire individual estates for the purpose of selling the items and making a profit) - this is what a liquidator could do for you. He or she would come in and offer you one price for everything. Pro: It gets everything sold and out of your restaurant quickly. Con: He or she will not offer you the best price. His or her bid will most likely be lower than what you could get out of the assets if you sold them yourself.

- **Develop a garage-sale mentality.** That probably sounds terrible to the person who has poured her life into a restaurant. However, as far as profits go, this is true. If you've ever had a garage sale, you know what this means. Disheartening but realistic. The same kinds of "profits" can be expected when you begin liquidating your restaurant's assets.

- **Have a private sale for employees.** You may have one or two employees who actually are trying to save up to start their own restaurant one day. If this is the case, they will pay more than garage-sale prices to begin stockpiling the things they'll need when they are ready to become restaurant owners. This may be one way for them to save money and for you to make a decent profit. It's worth a try.

- **Check with creditors to see if they will let you turn in assets for credit.** Some creditors and vendors will actually allow you to return assets for a partial (sometimes low) credit. They may be especially open to this idea if they deal in used equipment that they can then turn around and sell or lease to another restaurant.

- **Going-out-of-business - business sale.** A serious and humbling last-ditch effort to sell your business and provide continuing employment for your staff is possible. After you have developed your liquidation plan and know the dollar figure you are expecting to get out of the liquidation process, make a phone call to one of the potential buyers you were in negotiations with earlier. He or she may be willing to by the whole restaurant; lock, stock and barrel, now that the price has been so drastically reduced. This provides a way for you to get out quickly and not affect your employees. Yes - the buyer does make a killing on this one, so to speak. You only can select this option if you are a very confident person who can swallow your pride.

- **File all proper tax and legal documents.** There are tax responsibilities involved even when you liquidate your business. Actually, these tax documents might be good for you. But whether a gain or a loss is posted, don't forget to take care of any IRS business that is left undone after the closing of your restaurant. There may be also state, federal or local documents to file, depending on where your business is located. Don't forget to tie up these loose ends.

- **Close the business legally.** When you are filing documents and filling out IRS papers, be sure to officially and legally file the documents that will close the restaurant in the eyes of the legal system. If you have no intention of opening this business or another business in this name in the future, then there is no reason to keep the restaurant open, legally speaking. If you do, the business continues to be open to all sorts of problems including different kinds of litigation. If it is closed in your mind, make sure it's also closed in the minds of the IRS and government officials in your area.

You are buying the future.

CHAPTER SEVEN

ENSURING FUTURE SUCCESS

How Do I Project Future Sales?

Some of the ideas presented in this manual have alluded to decisions that you must make based on the future potential of the restaurant. These projections are actually important to both the buyer and the seller alike. But just how is it that you figure out what business might be like at a future date? One important avenue of information is market and competition surveys. Because an existing business has a sales history, it will most likely make predictions more credible than projections on a brand-new restaurant with no history. However, it is important for both sides that the projections be as credible as possible. That's where market and competition surveys come in handy. Consider the following when compiling a survey:

- **You are buying the future.** One often-misunderstood concept about purchasing a company is that you are not purchasing the sales volume of yesterday. You are actually buying its ability to generate a profit in the future. That's why future projections are crucial. The secret is this: don't skip the survey - it's that important.

- **Consider hiring a professional firm.** Whether you perform the survey yourself or hire a professional to do it, it will cost you money. While it's true that hiring a professional will be more expensive, it is also advisable. If you are not from the area where the restaurant is located, or if it is an area unfamiliar to you, it may be very time consuming and difficult to execute by yourself. Even if you are familiar with the area, a lot hinges on the results of this survey. You want to make sure it is done correctly. Buying a restaurant isn't going to be cheap. You may as well add another expense to your list and get it done right.

- **The bank will like it.** Banks and other lending institutions may not require this survey if you are buying an established restaurant. (It would definitely be a requirement for someone developing a new business from scratch.) But while the bank may not request it, they sure will like it. It makes the statement that you are organized, responsible and ready to own the restaurant. They will be impressed, and it may be one of the deciding factors in giving you the loan you need.

- **Economics 101.** We all learned the law of supply and demand in Economics 101. This is a real-world situation where supply and demand matters. A survey will help the future buyer to understand how much demand there will be for food and beverage products, as well as the supply that must be kept on hand to generate profit. Without this information, you'll go into your new restaurant with one hand tied behind your back.

- **Investors will keep their money without it.**
  Investors will keep their money if you cannot
  supply the detailed information that a market
  and competition survey provides. Enough said.

- **You'll find out who works near you.** The
  survey will supply you with information about
  major employers in your area. Use this
  information to draw business from these groups.
  For example, if a major employer in your area is
  prone to keeping employees well into the
  evening, target these employees for take-out or
  carry-out service. Offer specials for their
  employees only.

- **Pinpoint schools near you.** Students can be a
  major source of income for any food service
  establishment. The survey will let you know
  which schools are near. If a university is in your
  trading area, provide specials to attract these
  students and faculty. If a high school is in your
  trading proximity, find out if the school has an
  open-campus lunch policy. If it does, you'll be
  surprised at how many high school students will
  leave campus to eat out. Student-priced lunch
  deals with a student-friendly atmosphere will
  draw them in by the dozens.

- **Direct and indirect competition.** If you are
  going to win any kind of battle, you must
  understand the competition. This survey will
  give you information about the competing
  restaurants around you so that you can pull
  from their customer base. Study the information
  contained in this survey to learn the strengths

and weaknesses of your competitors. Become strong where they are weak, and strengthen yourself where they are already strong.

- **Major arterials will be outlined in the survey.** All the major traffic patterns in the area will be defined. Before purchasing any restaurant, make sure that traffic patterns will lend themselves to good business for you. For example, if you learn that a major interstate system is being developed that will remove half of your parking lot within the next five years, you might want to reconsider the purchase. Here's another example: A man purchased a restaurant right off a major freeway thinking it would give him access to all the people driving along that busy thoroughfare. What he did not realize was that, although he had visibility from the freeway, there were no exits within two miles of his establishment in either direction. It was just too hard to get off the freeway and then get turned around to eat at his establishment. It hurt his business dramatically.

- **Unemployment rate.** The market and competition survey will provide you with a pretty good picture of the unemployment rate in your area. If the unemployment rate is really high and the job market here does not appear to be improving in the near future, chances are unemployed people will not be eating out very often. Reconsider the purchase.

- **Nationalities and cultures.** You'll gain great insight into the nationalities and cultures represented in this geographic area. With this information, you can determine which type of restaurant might be most profitable. For example, if the area is highly populated with Hispanic Americans and you are considering purchasing a Mexican restaurant and cantina, chances are good that the restaurant will be successful.

- **The timing of customers.** This information will let you know the times of day customers actually arrive in the vicinity and are available to dine in your establishment. For example, the downtown areas of some cities are hopping well into the night. That's good for your dinner crowd. However, if the restaurant is located in an area that is vacated at five o'clock, and your big-ticket items are on the dinner menu, this may not be a good area for your type of restaurant.

- **Sell the parents.** The survey will give you all kinds of child-related information. For example, you will find out how many day care centers there are in the immediate area. If you find out that there are many day cares in your area, cater to those mothers. Single moms who are getting off work after a long day and really don't want to cook dinner will be enticed by a kids' dinner special. "Kids Eat Free" nights are also very successful.

- **Major attractions.** One patron in a Houston, Texas, restaurant was overheard making a comment about the establishment being a "gold mine." This particular restaurant happens to be located in an area surrounded by facilities that house concerts, rodeos, conventions and so on. When thousands of convention-goers attend these many different functions, nearby restaurants have standing-room-only crowds. Good location equals good crowds. The survey will give you this information.

Verify the Data

The following guidelines will give you some indication of the types of data that a market and competition survey may provide. This information is in no way complete and only represents some of the types of data received. Once this data has been received, it should be verified.

- **Go shopping.** A shopping spree in your trading area should confirm data compiled in the survey. For example, if the survey indicates a large population of children in the area, stores should reflect that with their available merchandise.

- **Make friends with a grocery store manager.** You can learn a lot about the available income in an area by the bag values of a local grocery store. A bag value is basically the grocery equivalent to an average tab (or check) at an eating establishment. High bag values indicate persons in the area may be more likely to eat out at full-service restaurants. Low bag values might be bad news for a full-service restaurant, but good news for the fast-food franchises. It's not difficult to get a grocery store manager to help you out if you explain who you are and why you want the information.

- **Take several walks, jogs and rides in the trading area.** You should personally take Sunday afternoon drives, long walks, jogs or bicycle rides all around the trading area to make sure the data collected appears to be consistent with your observations. If there seem to be numerous inconsistencies, you may want to consider redoing the survey.

- **Make a trip to the courthouse.** Any information regarding competitive restaurants that are opening in your trading area can be easily verified. Take a trip to the county courthouse (or other government building), and check to see if building permits, business licenses, food service licenses and licenses to sell alcohol all substantiate the data found in your survey.

- **Locate major destination points and businesses.** Locate the major businesses, tourist destinations, etc., that supposedly exist in your trading area. For example, if your survey indicates that a major employer such as Microsoft, NASA or Hewlett Packard is within miles of your proposed restaurant, make sure it's really there. If you are banking on Microsoft lunch crowds or late-night staffers at NASA, you'd better be sure they're really in your area.

Service After the Sale

Many of us have had the frustrating experience of purchasing a new vehicle amid the promises of service after the sale, just to find out that there was no service after purchase agreements were signed. They got their money; you got a lemon. Know the feeling? Selling your restaurant doesn't really require service from you later, unless you agreed to a partnership, management position or other place in the business. But nonetheless, you do have certain responsibilities after the sale. There are cases where the new owner doesn't want any help from you. But if the new owner does want or expect help from you, it is in your best interest to play your part.

- **Helping with a transition.** Most businesses will lose some of their customer base during a transition period. This can be especially true within the food service industry where the owner's personality may have played a big role in wooing patrons. It was mentioned earlier in this manual that having a transition team in place early on can actually be a great selling point. But as an ethical business man or woman, you really should make the transition more than a selling point. Make it a priority.

- **Be seen with the new owner.** Remembering that your legacy is at stake here, as well as your reputation, will help motivate you as you assist in the transition of your ownership to the new owner. One great way to make customers, employees and vendors feel comfortable is for them actually to see the new owner and the old owner working side by side. When this happens, they go from seeing just you to seeing you and the new owner to eventually seeing just the new owner. It's easier than seeing just you then just him. And it also makes your customers and employees feel like you didn't bail out on them. Leave gradually. Try it; it works.

- **Speak highly of the new owner, and do it often.** It is likely that you and this new owner may have had a few bumpy spots in the sales negotiations. Most sales have their bad moments, but the customers and employees should never know that. If they do, they may feel the need to take sides. You should speak very favorably of the new owner. Do it publicly as often as possible. This will not only speak highly of him or her; it will speak volumes about you.

- **Choose to dine in your old restaurant a few times following the sale.** If it was a very emotional sale for you, this may be difficult. But if you truly want what's best for your old restaurant and your employees, you'll grit your teeth and do it. If you are willing to choose this as a place you will dine, it will give a great boost to the "new guy."

- **Keep your attitude right if you still play a role in the business.** Some owners agree to a management position for an allotted number of years as part of the sales agreement. When this happens, it puts the old owner in a strange position. You go from being top dog to being an employee. If you are in this situation and you have problems with the new owner's choices, decisions, etc., keep it to yourself. Chances are you are only there for another two to three years. But these employees may be around for much longer. You don't have the right to force them to choose between you and the new owner. Be mature and keep your attitude to yourself.

- **Send a gift.** Wish the new owner well. Sounds a little mushy, huh? Keep in mind that you want this new owner to succeed. You want this restaurant that you started to continue. It speaks of your legacy. So you should publicly "bless" the new owner. A nice plant, a bottle of champagne, anything that says "Succeed. Good luck!" is appropriate. It's a nice gesture that will stand you in good stead. Also, remember that all these little nice things you are doing now can really pay off for you in the future if you decide to open a new business in this community. People remember nice gestures.

- **Give everyone a ride on a time machine.** When selling a restaurant, everyone involved may feel a little uneasy to begin with - employees, customers, vendors and so on. After all, everyone has a set routine, a favorite menu item, a required schedule. If you give them all a look into the future, they will feel more comfortable going into the whole thing. Make sure everyone knows what to expect.

- **Discuss management changes before the sale is final.** If either party desires any type of employment change, it should be discussed before the sale so that all employees are fairly taken care of in the transition. This is especially true for those employees in management positions. You want to make sure that people and their livelihoods are not "victims" of a sale. The best way to ensure this is to have everything included as a part of the purchase agreement.

- **Educate your customers.** You really must educate customers about what is happening, how it is going to happen and when they can expect it. This goes back to that gradual change mentality. As much as the new owner would like you to, you should continue to educate him or her after the sale. If the new owner does not want your input in this area, however, you must bow out gracefully.

- **Try not to change contact information.** If the restaurant had a phone number, Web address and other avenues of contact before you sold it, don't force a change with those contact numbers if at all possible. The business needs consistency. New phone numbers, Web addresses and so on make it more difficult for the new owner, customers and employees to carry on as usual.

Advice for the New Proprietor

Buying a restaurant may seem a little like a game of Hot Potato. You and several other buyers were all in the running during the negotiations, but somehow you landed the deal. It's natural to feel a little intimidated, scared or nervous as well as being excited about your new purchase. The following are some of the issues that you may need to address as you take over the helm at your food service establishment:

- **Make changes gradually.** It is natural to want to go in and make lots of changes. After all, you want to reflect who you are in this restaurant. That's important to you. You may even feel that some policies really need to be changed in order to realize the greatest profit for your business. But you must keep in mind that you are the new guy on the block. Customers, employees and vendors are still checking you out. Make changes gradually.

- **Speak well of the old owner.** Loyalty is a funny thing. You may have employees who didn't get along with the old guy, but somehow their loyalty is with him. Even though the food wasn't the best in this area, customers came out of loyalty. Vendors gave him great discounts because they were loyal to him, not to the restaurant. No matter what you think of his business skills, record-keeping ability, management ability or anything else, only speak highly of the old owner. Bad-mouthing him will cost you.

- **Don't kill the fun stuff.** The old owner gave away free beer with dinner every Friday night. When you start looking over the books, it seems like the expense of the Friday night beer is too high to maintain, so you kill it. But what was also the busiest, most profitable night of the week has now turned sour. You might not like the practice, but it's best to leave customer favorites in place until you can replace them with something better. The same is true for employee benefits. Let's say the old owners allowed each employee to have one free meal a day. You will want to carefully weigh the pros and cons of killing it before you do. A disgruntled employee is often an unproductive one. If the previous owner was very free in giving things away or loose in company policy, you may have to make some changes. But these changes should be made with care and over a long period of time.

- **Don't be afraid to change.** Just do it sensibly. When we talk about not killing fun stuff, it may sound as if you shouldn't change anything. You will have to change things to make this operation your baby. You may have ideas that will make the place better and more productive than it's ever been, but it's all in how you implement the changes. If you do it quickly, like a bull in a china shop, it will appear as if you have no regard for anyone other than yourself. Don't be afraid to change. Just remember to do it sensibly and gradually.

- **This acquisition should look like a timely**

haircut. Ever notice that if you allow your hair to grow and get shaggy before you finally get it cut, everyone notices. But if you always keep your hair clean-cut and cared for, nobody really notices that you got your haircut. A restaurant acquisition should be like a haircut. It should be so smooth that nobody really notices.

- **Meet with each employee personally.** Whether they are waitstaff, chefs, bartenders or whatever, meet with employees personally. If you acquired a company like IBM or Continental Airlines, that would be impossible. But the beauty of a restaurant is that meeting with each employee is a very doable thing. Listen to their concerns and their fears regarding this change. Share with them how you will make their job better for them. This personal touch will gain major points in the loyalty area. Take the time and do it.

- **Buy dinner, dessert or drinks for regular customers.** During the final sales and negotiation process, you really should have acquired a list of the restaurant's most regular customers. If you didn't get that list, get employees to help you put that information together now. Make a point to meet regular patrons and give them complimentary drinks, dessert or even a meal. It says you want to keep their business. You may take the financial hit now, but keeping their business can make you much more in the long run.

- **Get employee feedback on your one-month anniversary.** When you've been at the helm for about a month, have your employees give you feedback. You can do this in a staff meeting or even with confidential surveys. They will be able to see and hear things you can't. Pick up their knowledge and get them on your side in the process. (Everyone likes to be asked his or her opinion.)

- **Work long hours.** It probably goes without saying, but it will be important during the first six months that you develop personal relationships with key employees, customers and vendors. You can only do that if you're around during every shift. Plan on long hours now. It will help build a loyalty base and profit margin that will allow you to take a little time off later.

- **Have regular meetings with employees.** The previous owner may or may not have had regularly scheduled staff meetings. Consider having a weekly or monthly meeting during the first year of transition. The key to the success of these meetings is to make the employees a part of the meeting. It should not be a "chewing out" session to tell them what they've done wrong; it should be a time to encourage them, compliment them, pump them up and get their feedback. Be positive.

- **Evaluate current advertising campaigns.** A new owner probably is reason enough for a new ad campaign. Look at the advertising that is already in place (if at all), and go from there. If there is a catchy slogan that is well known in the community, you may not want to change that. But you can add to it, change colors, mediums of advertising and so on. Let the community know that something new and exciting is going on at your restaurant. Try offering coupons in print ads. It will bring in the people.

- **Address one employee complaint each month.** Whatever you can do without hurting your objectives, do it. It's an easy way to begin swinging employee loyalty over to you. And improvements like these will actually make things run more smoothly anyway.

- **Say thank you.** Those two little words mean a lot to people. It doesn't cost anything to utter those words, but the profit they can bring is phenomenal. Remember to say thank you to the employees who are working hard to make this transition work. Don't forget "thank you" for the regular customers who are sticking with you even though they loved the previous owner. And don't forget the vendors and community leaders who are standing behind you. It's an inexpensive way to get people on your side. Do it today.

Closing Thoughts

Whether you are buying, selling or leasing a restaurant, this manual has hopefully given you insight into the process that will help to secure the best deal for your situation. We leave you with a few last thoughts from the bottom of the chili bowl:

- **Go with your gut.** No matter if you are the buyer, seller, franchisee, landlord or whoever, go with your gut feelings. If everything looks good but something inside is telling you to stop the deal, you may want to halt everything. Go with your gut.

- **Hire an attorney.** Vital. Don't try to do this kind of a deal by yourself. Hire an attorney.

- **Don't buy someone else's disaster.** Name association is critical to the life of a business. If someone is trying to sell you a restaurant that has a bad name in the community, stay away from it. It would be easier to start your own from scratch than to overcome a bad name.

- **Set a deadline.** Don't let the selling process drag on forever. That's not good for you, your employees or your restaurant. If you're having trouble selling, set a deadline and stick to it. If you haven't sold by that time, consider some other option.

- **Have fun.** Whether you are buying or selling, have fun. This could be the business deal of a lifetime. It could be the fulfillment of a lifelong dream. Don't get so bogged down in the process that you miss the excitement in it. Have fun!

INDEX

401K, 89

A
accountants, 48
acquisition, 135
advertising, 64, 137
alterations, 83
appraiser, 42
asking price, 29, 110
assets, 12, 35
attorney, 12, 24, 28
attorney fees, 48
auction, 20

B
bar supplies, 48
beer, 48
beverages, 48
bookkeepers, 48
broker, 20, 31, 72
business plan, 75
buyer, 14, 18, 26, 30, 46
buyout, 68

C
capital gain, 101
cash, 29

Caveat emptor, 107
collateral, 30
common sense, 13
competition, 23, 55
condemnation, 84
confidentiality agreement, 22, 96
cost approach, 39
costs, 52
covenants, 104
credit report, 74
creditors, 120
customers, 69, 136

D
delegate, 17, 114
deposit, 85
disclosure, 26, 99
down payment, 90
due diligence, 95

E
electricity, 49
employee stock option plan, 116
employees, 35, 111, 119, 137

environmental issues, 98
Equifax, 74
escrow, 29
expenses, 41, 49
Experian, 74
exterminator, 49

F
facilitator, 22
fees, 91
financial statements, 36
financing, 57
fixtures, 53
food, 47
franchise, 51
franchise rule, 63
franchisee, 62, 65, 66
franchising, 54
franchising checklist, 59
franchisor, 59
future sales, 123

G
goals, 10, 19
goodwill, 41

I
income, 41
income approach, 39
indemnification, 104
inheritance, 89
insurance, 48, 84
International Franchise
Association, 57
inventory, 38
IRS, 101

L
landlord, 69, 75, 81
lawyer, 78
lease, 68, 73, 77
lease broker, 71
leasehold terms, 41
leases, 67
letter of intent, 76
letter of reference, 75
leveraged buy out, 116
licenses, 49
liquidation, 112
listing brokers, 71
loan, 47
location, 35

M
maintenance, 85
management buy out, 116
market approach, 39
marketing, 35
memorandums, 23
middleman, 20
motive, 43

N
negotiate, 16, 43
negotiator, 73

non-capital improve ments, 81

O
offer, 25
owner, 36

P
paperwork, 27
parking, 83
partners, 89, 92
patience, 17
payroll, 47
petty cash, 91
policy manual, 31
preparation, 31
price, 36
priorities, 15
profitability, 40
proprietor, 134
prospectus, 34, 37

R
real estate, 41
references, 71
rent, 47
repairs, 15
rule-of-thumb pricing, 42

S
seller, 46, 94, 108
selling, 32
selling principles, 18
shareholder, 103

Small Business Administration, 57, 87
stock market, 11
stock options, 44
stocks, 44, 89
sublet, 67

T
tax returns, 75
taxes, 99
telephone, 49
term, 83
track record, 40
trademark, 63
training, 53
Trans Union, 74
transition, 24

U
union, 23
utilities, 84

V
verbal, 27

W
warranties, 104
wine, 48
writing, 27

Y
Yellow Pages, 12

If you enjoy ~~~~ entire series!

The
FOOD Service Professional
GUI

647
.95
An

3860252

Andrews, Lynda.

Buying & selling a
restaurant business,
for maximum profit.

$19.95

		DATE	FEB 1 7 2004

Qty	Or		Total
	Ite		
	Ite		
	Ite		
	Ite		
	Ite		
	Ite		
	Ite		
	Ite		
	Ite		
	Ite		
	Ite		
	Ite		
	Ite		
	Ite		
	It		
	It		
	It		

SHIP TO

Name_____

Company Nam

Mailing Addre

City _____

FAX _____

❏ My check or ~ is attached

❏ Please char

Card # ☐ ☐

Please ma ~ 4474-7014
USI ~ et.

BAKER & TAYLOR